GRACE ERREA AND MERIDITH OSTERFELD

IMPRESSIONIST
A P P L I Q U É

Exploring Value & Design to Create Artistic Quilts

C&T PUBLISHING

Text and Photography copyright © 2012 by Grace Errea and Meridith Osterfeld

Photography and Artwork copyright © 2012 by C&T Publishing, Inc.

Photography copyright © 2012 by Dan Snipes

Publisher: Amy Marson

Creative Director: Gailen Runge

Acquisitions Editor: Susanne Woods

Editors: Phyllis Paoli and Liz Aneloski

Technical Editors: Sandy Peterson and Amanda Siegfried

Cover/Book Designer: April Mostek

Production Coordinator: Jessica Jenkins

Production Editor: S. Michele Fry

Illustrator: Lon Eric Craven

Photography by Christina Carty-Francis and Diane Pedersen of C&T Publishing, Inc., unless otherwise noted

Published by C&T Publishing, Inc., P.O. Box 1456, Lafayette, CA 94549

Library of Congress Cataloging-in-Publication Data

Errea, Grace, 1944-

Impressionist appliqué : exploring value & design to create artistic quilts / Grace Errea & Meridith Osterfeld.

   p. cm.

ISBN 978-1-60705-467-2 (soft cover)

1. Quilting. 2. Appliqué. 3. Color in textile crafts. I. Osterfeld, Meridith, 1943- II. Title.

TT835.E77 2012

746.46--dc23

2011026255

Printed in China

10 9 8 7 6 5 4 3 2 1

Photo by Dan Snipes

Dedication

We dedicate this book to the intrepid souls everywhere who are ready to explore and find the creative art quilter within.

Acknowledgments

To the wonderful students who constantly teach us as much as or more than we teach them, and to all the students who so generously contributed their artwork for this book, a heartfelt thank-you! Thanks also to our dear friends Jean Selner and Ingrid Stuiver, who so kindly agreed to be our "guinea pigs" to see if they could make sense of our ramblings and instructions.

From Grace: To my husband, Mack, and our daughters, Julie and Lauren, and Julie's husband, Jean-Paul—thank you for your enthusiasm, ongoing support, and encouragement. To Thelma and Louise, our cat-kids, and to Kizzie, Jamie, and Jessie before them—you've given us such enjoyment and love and have been the inspiration for some of my quilts. To my co-author, Meridith—it's a darn good thing that one of us likes to write! To the members of the Beach Cities Quilters Guild—your friendship, encouragement, and sharing have helped immensely.

From Meridith: To my husband, Hank—thank you for your patience, my wonderful quilt studio, putting up with my quirks, and understanding my need to "season" all that fabric in my stash. To my children (and their spouses), Sage (Terri), Brett (Katja), Kate, and Justin (Kristen)—thank you for your support, understanding, and amusement with my passion for "cutting perfectly good big pieces of material into little pieces and then sewing them together again." To my nine wonderful grandchildren, Season, Tristan, Tierin, Griffin, Hope, Shylee, Makenna, Cash, and Dylan—you make me smile, and I love you not only for who you are but also because you love my quilts, "warts and all." To Grace—your artistic talent and quilts inspire me, and so many others, and give us hope! Your patience, teaching talent, and help make it all "do-able."

From both of us: Thank you to the entire C&T family for believing in us. We appreciate your help, your empathy, and all that you did to ensure that the process was enjoyable and fulfilling. Our thanks to acquisitions editor Suzanne Woods for encouraging us and welcoming us to the C&T family; creative director Gailen Runge for answering endless questions; publisher Amy Marson for patiently helping make sense of the "legalese"; developmental editor Phyllis Paoli for constructive comments, thoughtful insights, and support; senior developmental editor Liz Aneloski for helping us with logistics and making some tough decisions; production editor Michele Fry, production coordinator Jessica Jenkins, illustrator Lon Eric Craven, and cover/designer April Mostek, whose creativity made this the art and quilt book we hoped it would be. To our technical editors, Sandy Peterson and Amanda Siegfried—your thoughtfulness, attention to detail, and positive observations were appreciated. We thoroughly enjoyed the wonderful experience it has been working with all of you.

Contents

Project Quilts

Celebrating Your Journey   87

About the Authors   95

INTRODUCTION:
Exploring Value—The Secret of Stunning Art Quilts

Setting out to create a quilt is like embarking on a journey, an exploration into the land of creativity. The resulting art piece allows us to depict and share our visions and dreams. This book is an invitation for you to join in this journey. The trip we take together will be an adventure into a new and tactile way of interpreting the world and art through fiber, in a manner that is both contemporary and realistic. It will be a sensual experience, one of texture, light and shadow, and emotion. In the process, we hope to show you a more sophisticated way of using simple techniques and tools to create your own elegant textile art.

Although photos and other art provide inspiration, appliqué is used to create the quilts. This is not primarily a book about either photo quilts or appliqué. Rather, it is about the importance of *value* in art quilts. Part of the secret of creating showstopping art quilts is correctly interpreting value instead of adhering strictly to nature's hues. Art becomes more interesting, creative, and personal—and far more sophisticated— when you move beyond making strict reproductions of nature and instead "walk on the wild side."

Color is an important component in art quilts, but from our perspective, value is primary and hue is secondary. Therefore the focus of our artistic journey is on the importance of value. Our hope is that through this process you will develop a new appreciation for the world around you and the important role that value plays in art.

Photo by Dan Snipes

EL JEFÉ, 36" × 44", by Grace Errea

A note about the voice throughout this book: Grace is the artistic inspiration behind the quilts in this book, so hers is the "I" voice that explains processes and shares ideas. Meridith is the writer, idea person, and "translator" of Grace's artistic vision. Together, we work as a collaborative team.

TOUCAN, 52″ × 66″, by Grace Errea

Planning *for* Your Journey

"A journey of a thousand miles begins with a single step."

—*Lao-tzu (Chinese proverb)*

MASAI FAMILY PORTRAIT, 52″ × 42″, by Grace Errea

Whether a journey is going to be an extensive one or just a weekend sojourn, before you take a single step it's generally a good idea to put some thought into preparing for the trip. The same thing is true for setting out on a journey as an art quilter. The following pages present an overview of the essentials you need to think about so your journey will be a successful one.

The Elements of Art

> "*Line* gives you *shape*. Through the use of *value*, shape gives you *form*, which is enhanced by the use of *texture* and *color*."
>
> —*Professor Vito-Leonardo (Lenny) Scarola, Saddleback College Department of Art, Mission Viejo, California*

The basic elements of art include line, shape, value, form, texture, and color. Although all of these are essential in an art piece, for us, as quilters, what really transforms these elements into art is *value*—the lightness or darkness of the colors we mix in our fabric compositions.

Line

Lines on a quilt can be created in different ways. Strips of fabric can be cut in straight or wavy lines, or in a combination of the two, and arranged on a background—negative space, in art terminology. Negative space is the empty space around shapes and forms; positive space is where shapes and forms exist.

Place two or more shapes together on a quilt, and they create a line where they abut or overlap. The prominence of these lines and shapes is directly related to their value—their lightness or darkness—and to how much contrast there is between them. The greater the difference in value, the more prominent the lines.

Photo by Grace Errea

The house is an example of *lines* combined and arranged on negative space (background) creating *shapes* and *forms* or positive space.

Photo by Dan Snipes

Lines can be seen between the apple and its leaves, its stem, and the background. On the apple's surface, sunlight and shading form lines. Highlights from the sun make more lines on the leaves and the stem.

Shape

When you close a meandering line, you create a shape that has two dimensions: height and width.

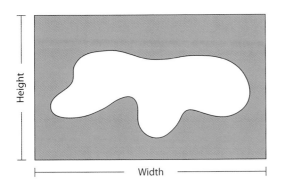

When you cut fabric so that it forms a shape and then combine that shape with other shapes on a background, the way you arrange them, and their value and color differentials, influences which way the eye moves and what the brain perceives.

In *The Bracelet*, the hand is intentionally arranged diagonally from left to right, moving the eye onto the figure and directing it upward. The hand stands out against the plain blue-gray color of the shawl, while the scarf's bold colors attract the eye upward to the face. The calm, neutral background focuses the viewer's attention on the figure—in particular, on the face, the scarf, and the hand.

Photo by Dan Snipes

THE BRACELET, 32" × 37", by Grace Errea

Form

Three-dimensional forms have height, width, and depth. How can we add the perception of a third dimension—depth—to a two-dimensional quilt surface? That's where value comes in. We can use the juxtaposition of lightness and darkness to create the perception of proximity or distance, adding a sense of three-dimensional form to a two-dimensional art piece.

Photo by Grace Errea

A two-dimensional shape looks three dimensional with the addition of light and shadow.

An artist working with pigments, charcoal, or graphite can easily make small gradations in value or color by blending and smudging. That's what creates a sense of form. But it isn't quite that simple with fabrics.

In the drawing of the apple, realistic gradation was achieved with a Conté stick or crayons (a drawing medium of charcoal or graphite mixed with wax and clay). Pigments, charcoal, or graphite can easily be added, blended, or smudged to make small changes in the gradation of value or color. Blending fabrics can be difficult because of the nature of the medium. Although gradual changes in color or value can be achieved with fabric, it is more difficult, and there is always a line, however subtle.

The apple on the left is a Conté crayon drawing. The one on the right is made of fabric.

Texture

The "feel," or perceived surface quality, of an object (rough, smooth, soft) is texture. Our eyes and brain cooperate with our sense of touch so that we feel the up-and-down surface texture of a woven item, such as a wicker basket. Through the strategic use of line, value, and hue, that same texture can be *implied* in basket weave–patterned material.

A bath towel has real texture that you can feel. Even if the image of a bath towel were transferred onto a smooth piece of cotton fabric, you'd probably still think it looks nubby and soft. Experience tells us that stones may be rough and have irregular edges. On fabric, these qualities can be implied through the use of value, hue, and irregular lines.

Real—Terrycloth   Implied—Basket weave   Implied—Stone

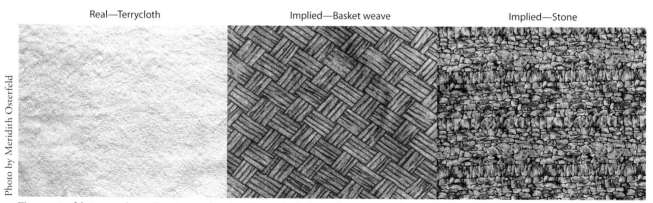

Texture in fabric may be real, or it may be visually implied through pattern and color.

The Components of Color

When most people speak of color, they are thinking only of hue. But color actually has three major components: hue, saturation, and value. *Hue* is the family in which a color is grouped. *Saturation* is the amount of the color in a sample. *Value* is a color's lightness or darkness. Early in my quilting journey, I recognized that hue was an important factor in quilt design and creation. However, right from the beginning of that journey, I felt that value was of even greater importance. When I am designing a quilt, I first determine what values I will use, and then I decide on colors.

Objects have no color of their own; rather, they reflect or absorb different wavelengths of light. White light (sunlight) consists of the seven hues of the rainbow: red, orange, yellow, green, blue, indigo, and violet. An object's hue is named according to which of these are reflected by the object. White is what we see when all the colors are reflected. Black is what we perceive when all the colors are absorbed. We see a specific color when some light waves are reflected and others are not.

Hue

Each hue is a specific wavelength of light that is reflected differently than any other hue. When we label a color, we are naming it according to its color family—red, for instance. To further distinguish between the different family members, we give them second names. For instance, we can distinguish among reds by referring to them as rose red, burgundy red, or scarlet red. In practical terms, hue and color are used interchangeably.

Saturation

> "The purity or the strength of a color is its saturation. Saturation is the amount of gray in any specific color."
>
> —*Online Literacy Project at Pomona College, Brian Stonehill's Spring 1994 Media 51 Principles of Visual Literacy (saturation credit Ann Oelschlager, Elena Villegas, Anjali Satyu)*

When a hue contains virtually no gray, it is considered a highly saturated and "pure" color. Saturation doesn't change the basic hue or its value: Green remains green; red is still red. The value—lightness or darkness—stays the same, because any gray that's added or removed has the same value as the original hue. When you add gray, there is simply less color and more gray, making the color less and less prominent until it becomes *desaturated* and just looks gray.

Photo by Meridith Osterfeld

From left to right, these colors are fully saturated (little to no gray) to desaturated (values of gray only).

Another way to desaturate is to add black or white to a pure color. Adding black produces *shades*, while adding white produces *tints*. Either way, the amount of pure color decreases, and the value of the original hue changes.

Photo by Meridith Osterfeld

At left, white has been added to the parrot's red, creating a tint of the original coloration in the center photo. At right, the red has been shaded with the addition of black.

Value

Value is the lightness or darkness of a hue. In an art class, I created a Ten-Value Gray Scale that ranges from white to black in ten steps. Starting with both white and black paints, I mixed pigments by adding drops of the opposite color (black to white and white to black). I painted a tiny chip for each new combination, ending up with hundreds of chips. With my instructor's assistance, I selected ten chips that represented a smooth transition from white to black.

When I took my gray scale home to use in my quilting, I removed the white and the black ends, leaving me with eight values. I also renumbered these eight values from 1 to 8 in my Eight-Value Gray Scale, because for my purposes, all white and all black remain outside my working gray scale. Then I matched my gray quilting fabrics to the Eight-Value Gray Scale and made a second gray scale from gray fabrics.

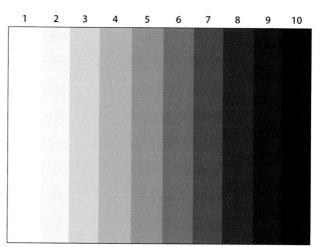

Ten-Value Gray Scale

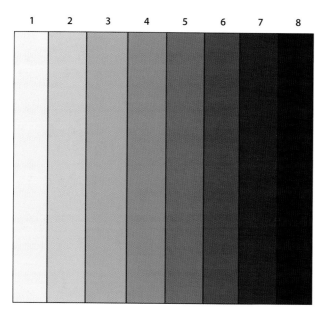

Eight-Value Gray Scale

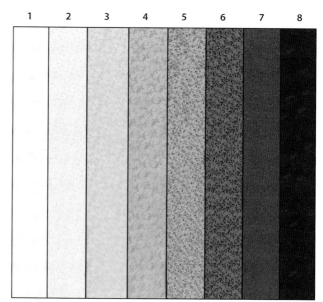

Fabric version of the Eight-Value Gray Scale

Understanding Value in Color

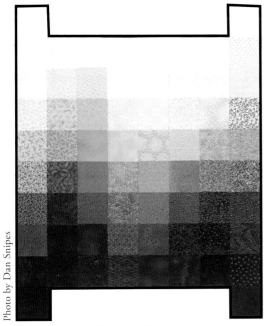

Photo by Dan Snipes

Periodic Table of Value in Color

After making the gray scale, I expanded the scale to include the eight values of each primary and secondary color—red, orange, yellow, green, blue, and violet. In the Periodic Table of Value in Color, each column represents the gradual transition of a color from its lightest tint (white with a hint of color) to its darkest shade (black with a hint of color). In these color columns, the starting and ending points (white and black) were left off because the assumption is that all start with white and end with black. White and black are left only in the gray column and in the black and white column to give the table its distinctive "H" shape, making it reminiscent of science's Periodic Table of the Elements. The black-and-white column was added because using small prints in black and white makes them appear as a single color when viewed from a distance.

The table shows eight columns with values increasingly darker from top to bottom. To get a better comparison between values in color, I used the gray scale as a base in the first column. It is much easier to read the value of gray, because gray lacks intensity (brightness or dullness), color, and temperature (cool/warm colors). These elements can be distracting when determining the value of a color. Each color swatch is compared to the gray column to assign a value.

The first complete horizontal row (left to right) has the lightest values in all colors—white with a touch of the color. The eighth row has the darkest values in all colors—black with a touch of the color. The table does not include "neutral" colors such as beige or ecru because the neutrals used in my quilts are generally subsets of one of the primary or secondary colors, such as orange or yellow.

Value in Color

Knowing the values of your fabrics and how to use them in your quilts is essential in creating convincing images in art quilts. The Periodic Table of Value in Color can help make sense of it all by giving you a way to figure out values.

Midrange colors

Midrange colors are the most intensely saturated with color. On the table, they fall in either the fourth or fifth row, depending on their intensity (brightness or dullness).

Midrange colors

Tints

Tints are derived when white is added to saturated colors, making them lighter than the original colors. The table's Value 1, Value 2, and Value 3 rows are tints. Each successive row is slightly more saturated with color than the one above it.

Tints

Shades

Adding black to saturated color produces shades. Though shades are darker than the original hues, they are less saturated with pure color because the black dilutes them. The last three rows in the table (Values 6, 7, and 8) get increasingly darker, but each row is less saturated with pure color than the row above it because it contains more black.

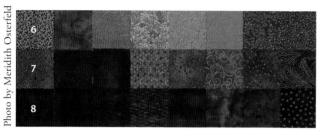

Shades

Tones

A fourth group of colors is tones, a subset of the previous three groups (midrange, tints, and shades). A tone is any color to which gray *of the same value as the original hue* has been added. Tones do not appear as a separate category in the table because they are simply a subset of individual table colors with varying amounts of gray added. In the photo below, the midrange Value 4 and Value 5 colors have been slightly desaturated with the addition of gray, creating tones.

Toned midrange colors

Toned hues are desaturated because there is less of the pure hue in the mix. Tones can have any value; they can be tints, midrange colors, or shades. The new color is the same hue and value as the original, as long as the added gray has the same value.

Toned green fabrics are shown behind more saturated counterparts of the same value: tints (left), midrange (center), and shades (right).

Value Is Relative

A color's lightness or darkness may be perceived differently depending on its surroundings. A fabric that seems light when surrounded by darker fabrics may look dark when surrounded by lighter fabrics.

Relative values shift—often dramatically—depending on the "neighborhood." Follow the small squares in the photo from left to right, noticing how they appear to change value. Although the squares at the top (Value 8), middle (Value 4), and bottom (Value 1) don't actually change, they *appear* lighter or darker in comparison to their surroundings.

- The top dark square looks very dark against the lightest background, but it virtually disappears against the darkest background.

- The middle square looks dark against the lightest background, almost disappears in the middle, and appears light against the darkest background.

- The bottom square is almost indistinguishable from the lightest background. By the time it is shown against the darkest background, it looks very light and quite prominent in comparison.

You can see the same value-shifting phenomenon when a blue Value 5 square is displayed against a range of blue backgrounds. The square is most distinct and has the clearest edges on backgrounds with Values 1–3.

Although it's discernable on other backgrounds, it doesn't look quite as sharp as it does against the lighter values.

The perception of value can also depend on color. Some hues have intrinsic lightness or darkness. Warm colors and very bright colors fool the eye into thinking they are lighter in value than they actually are. The photo below shows only midrange colors, yet some look lighter or brighter than others.

This perception becomes noticeable when you desaturate colors by converting them to gray. The same image reproduced in gray scale shows that the warm colors (red, oranges, and yellows) look noticeably lighter or darker than their gray scale counterparts in the cool colors.

Using Value

Knowing how to use value will enable you to create magical quilts filled with convincing images. Value, hue, and shape are the three elements to focus on the most, with value always being the most important. Value is the first choice you should make in designing a quilt. With values decided, most designs can be created in any hue. Value is what does most of the work in art quilts, even though hue usually gets most of the credit.

Gradations in value can be used to give emphasis, to form a focal point, or to create the impression that something has depth and dimension. You can even use value to establish a time of day or to set a mood.

Creating a Focal Point

Using value differentials is one of the most effective ways to create a dramatic center of attention, or a focal point, in any design. The greater the difference in value between a focal point and its surroundings, the more prominent it will be.

Because value is relative to its surroundings, a dark form on a light background immediately becomes the center of attention, as illustrated in *Morning Glory* by Linda Hannawalt. (For step-by-step instructions for making *Morning Glory,* see pages 35–49.)

Detail from *MORNING GLORY* by Linda Hannawalt

Conversely, a light form on a dark background also seems to "pop out," as you can see from Monica Schurter's interpretation of the same quilt. To ensure that an area becomes a focal point, there should be a differential of at least two or three values, making the edges appear sharp against the background.

Detail from *MORNING GLORY by Monica Schurter*

Color contrast also helps create an area of interest. Hues that are opposite one another on the color wheel (complementary colors such as red and green or violet and yellow) produce high contrast and draw the viewer's eye. Warm hues like red, orange, and yellow get attention because they appear to be closer to the viewer, while cool hues such as green, blue, and violet appear to recede.

The higher the contrast and the greater the difference in value between the elements in your composition, the more dramatic the outcome will be.

Creating a Three-Dimensional Appearance

You can make your two-dimensional shapes appear three dimensional through the use of differing values.

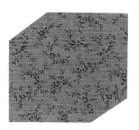
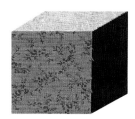
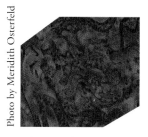

Each pair of shapes uses the same hues, but varying the surface values makes the blocks on the right more accurately depict three-dimensional objects.

Lighter values give the impression that the light portion is "on top," or is closer to the light source and to the viewer. Conversely, darker values juxtaposed with lighter ones appear to be shadowed and receding from the viewer.

As shown in the above photograph, the illusion of depth in a field may be created in a number of ways:

- Make background items smaller and foreground items larger. The shrubs in the foreground appear considerably larger than those in the background. Some of them actually look larger than the distant hills, making the hills seem farther away. Larger objects draw more attention when surrounded with smaller ones and vice versa.

- Clear hues (not toned with gray) with high color saturation seem closer to the viewer when paired with more tinted or shaded hues.

- The sharper an object and the clearer its edges, the more prominent it is—especially if other objects in the picture have softer edges or are out of focus.

- Lighter values and toned (grayed) hues for background shapes give the appearance that they are receding. This is called *atmospheric perspective* because you are viewing the objects as though through hazy air.

Creating a Reflection

A reflection is a phenomenon caused by the change of direction when a wave moves from one medium to another. An echo is one example. A reflection in water is another. A reflection in water occurs when a light wave moving through the air changes direction after it hits the denser medium of water. The light bounces off, hits an object (a boat or a swan, for example), and returns to the water. The water stops the light wave, and we see a mirror image of the object—a reflection.

Reflections may be toned or colored by the water itself. The surroundings—the sky, for instance, or plants—might make water look blue, aqua, green, gray, black, gold, or reddish. Clear and particularly deep water may appear to be black or very deep blue. Sand or soil may color water brown or yellow.

SWAN LAKE, 51" × 37", by Grace Errea

The reflection of the light-colored swan is two values darker than the focal point.

Re-creating a reflection's value with textiles is a lot like mixing paint. You look for a value somewhere in between that of your focal point and the water to create a realistic reflection, auditioning fabrics to see what works. The hues themselves remain the same, unless you exercise some artistic license.

CYGNUS NEGRA, 31" × 25", by Grace Errea

The reflection of the dark focal point was achieved by using a toned fabric three values lighter than that of the swan.

Establishing Time of Day and Conveying a Mood

Another important use of value is establishing a time of day or conveying a mood. Different times of day evoke different feelings in people. We often think of sunrise as a quiet time before the bustle of the day begins. Sunset seems like a winding-down time, and moonlight is associated with love and romance.

Both value and hue can help establish a time of day. What colors do you associate with early morning? I tend to think of a world of tints, with soft shadows and pastels of pink, peach, aqua, gray, gold, and blue. Sunsets are crimson, gold, magenta, lavender, and purple. Moonlit nights are creamy or stardust white, dark velvet blue, and inky black. It may be different for you. In general, though, most of us think of midrange hues as lively, tints as soft and serene, and shades as quieting or mysterious.

In the two photos, the sun isn't far from the horizon. Both photos use similar hues but in very different values. In the first image, strong midrange colors and shades convey the feeling of lengthening shadows and a setting sun. It is hot, fiery, and spectacular—rich in drama. In general, shades and highly saturated hues can evoke a sense of high drama, romance, and intrigue.

Photo by Grace Errea

The lighter, softer tints in the second image evoke a more serene and calm feeling. The scene is now reminiscent of the mists of an early morning, when the sun has just come over the horizon.

Photo by Grace Errea

Knowing the value of your fabrics and how to use them in your quilts is essential in creating convincing images and sensational quilts.

LIFE AFTER THE STORM, 49" × 51", by Grace Errea

Preparing *and* Organizing Tools *and* Supplies

*Y*ou've decided to set out on a quilting journey. It's time to prepare for your trip! This chapter includes a checklist of essential supplies for creating art quilts, along with three activities—one to help you organize your fabrics, and two to prepare the tools you'll need.

The first activity, Organizing Your Stash, is invaluable in helping you create art pieces that have a three-dimensional perspective. You'll be able to quickly choose the right values for the patterns in this book as well as for your own designs. The other two activities, making two variations of a Periodic Table of Value in Color and then a Color/ Value Fan, will provide you with the perfect carry-along tools.

JESSIE, 33½" × 36½", by Grace Errea

19

ESSENTIAL SUPPLIES

You'll use the following tools and supplies throughout your journey as an art quilter.

Backing fabric for quilts

Batting

Bobbins (prefilled with clear nylon)

Cotton swabs (We prefer Q-tip brand.)

Craft knife (such as an X-Acto knife)

Double-stick fusible webbing (optional) (We prefer Steam-A-Seam 2.)

Embellishments—beads and yarn (optional)

Fabric glue (We prefer Roxanne's Glue-Baste-It.)

Foam core board, 30″ × 40″ (or as specified for the activity or project)

Freezer-paper roll, 18″ wide

Painter's multiuse tape or masking tape

Pens—Sharpie black permanent marker with fine point and ultrafine point; ballpoint

Pencils—erasable red and blue

Pins of several types (1″–1½″ extra-thin silk pins, flower-head, or other decorative-head pins; T-pins; and 1″–1½″ quilting safety pins)

Poster board, 3 pieces white, 22″ × 28″

Quilting gloves

Quilting rulers (6″–12″ and 18″–24″, 12½″ square, 2″ square)

Rotary cutter and mat

Scissors for fabric and small, sharp scissors for paper

Seam ripper

Self-adhesive laminated sheets (optional)

Self-threading needles for hand sewing

Spray bottle for water

Spray sizing light fabric finish

Spray starch

Stabilizer material (We use petticoat netting, which is not as stretchy or flimsy as tulle and not as stiff or heavy as regular netting. Also, the hole size is different.)

Stiffener (such as Fray Block by June Tailor)

Stiletto

Thread—nylon invisible in clear and smoke colors; 50-weight cotton in light beige and dark gray or other neutral colors (if your bobbin won't accept nylon thread); rayon and metallic thread for embellishing (optional); 50-weight cotton for quilting the projects; water-soluble basting thread (We prefer Wash-A-Way thread by YLI.)

Vinyl, clear (such as a painter's drop cloth or a tablecloth, 1–2mm thick, as specified for individual projects)

Your tone-on-tone fabric collection (page 21)

BASIC SUPPLIES

Envelopes (for storing pattern pieces)

Eraser

Iron and ironing board

Long-handled tweezers

Sewing machine with free-motion (darning) and open-toe (embroidery) feet; ¼″ walking foot (optional)

Sewing machine needles (universal 60/8 or 65/9 or 70/10, and 80/12)

Ahhh! Fabrics

One of the most enjoyable experiences a quilt artist has is purchasing fabrics. Shopping for fabric is both a visual and a sensual experience. You not only receive visual stimulation from all those colors and patterns, but you also get to use your tactile senses as you feel the fabrics and savor their textures.

Buy good-quality 100% cotton fabric. It's worth it! Select quarter-yard cuts, fat quarters or fat eighths, and scraps for the tone-on-tone fabric collection that is the basis of any art quilt. You'll also need larger pieces for backgrounds (unless you are planning to piece them), a large piece for backing each quilt, and a piece for binding. Check the individual quilt sizes and patterns to determine how much you need.

> *Most fabric manufacturers keep fabrics available for only a limited time, so if you really like a particular fabric, buy a few yards for your stash.*
>
> TIP

Tone-on-Tone Fabrics

Tone-on-tone fabric has a closely spaced design or pattern that's not high in contrast with the background or other designs in the pattern. Often the "pattern" is just a different value or a neighboring hue, giving the fabric the overall appearance of being a single color when it's viewed from a distance.

You'll need small pieces of tone-on-tone fabrics in many colors and values for the projects in this book.

Tone-on-tone fabric in geometrics, florals, and batiks

Other Fabrics

Blending is a key element in art quilts. You don't want one fabric or shape to stand out so much that it actually distracts the viewer from seeing your quilt as a whole. Solid-colored material, for example, tends to have a flat appearance that looks out of place among tone-on-tone fabrics.

Fabrics with obvious designs, such as these distinctive checks and novelty prints, don't work well in art quilts.

With black-and-white fabric, you have either a black print on white or a white print on black. When the amounts of black and white are roughly equal, you get midrange values. With more white and less black, the overall value becomes a tint; more black and less white gives you a shade. Small-scale prints in black and white can work as tone-on-tone fabrics, but large-scale prints are too widely spaced to give an overall tone-on-tone appearance and will call too much attention to themselves.

Black-and-white prints can be considered tone-on-tone if the pattern is small and closely spaced.

Gray is not the same as black and white, even though a black-and-white fabric may read as a gray if the scale and proportion are right. Black-and-white prints are distinctively black and white.

Photo by Meridith Osterfeld

Gray tone-on-tone fabric has different values of gray on a gray background.

Fabric Preparation

Prewash your fabrics to test for and control colorfastness and shrinkage, as well as to remove chemicals. Although you will rarely wash an art quilt, you will generously wet it in some steps of construction. Because some fabrics bleed, it is important to remove excess color before using the fabric in your quilt. Reds, purples, and blues are especially prone to bleeding. Also, all-cotton fabric may be prone to shrinking. Washing first will help control both shrinkage and bleeding.

Wash your fabric in warm water and partially dry it on a low setting. (Do not use dryer softener sheets or liquid fabric softener—they make the fabric harder to handle.) Hang the still-damp fabric to finish drying it, and then fold and store it. When you are ready to use it, press the amount you need, using light spray sizing to give it more body and to make it easier to handle. (You'll find the sizing near the spray starch in most stores.)

Fraying and tangling of threads is natural with some fabrics. Washing fabric in a lingerie bag or pillowcase, or snipping off the corners diagonally before washing, may help limit fraying. If fabric does fray, cut off the loose threads when you take it out of the washing machine.

Fabric Grain

Lengthwise-grain threads run the length of the fabric, parallel to the selvage, and are the strongest and most stable. Crosswise-grain threads, which run from one selvage to the other, are less stable and tend to stretch. Bias grain is cut at a 45° angle to the selvage. When you cut on the bias, you must handle the fabric carefully, because the bias edge will be extremely stretchy. Bias edges fray less than fabric cut on the straight of the grain, and their give makes them great for curvy shapes such as flower stems.

Don't worry about cutting or sewing on any particular grain, but do bear in mind that some pieces may be on the bias, so you need to treat them gently. Handle all pieces minimally, and never iron with a back-and-forth motion! Press only, using an up-and-down motion (contact on down, no contact on up), as opposed to "ironing" back and forth.

Fussy Cutting for Directional Fabric

You may decide that fabric with a directional pattern is the best choice for a particular shape. Position your template so that the pattern in the fabric enhances the appearance of the shape. Then fussy cut to make the best use of the fabric design.

In this directional fabric, which was chosen for leaf shapes, the lighter-value lines give the appearance of veins and have a strong directional flow.

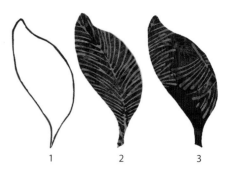

A leaf shape (1) at left makes optimal use of the fabric pattern (2) in the center example. The placement at right (3) is not the best use of the directional pattern.

Stabilizer

I use what is referred to as "petticoat netting"—not regular netting or tulle—as a stabilizer for my quilts. This material is inexpensive and readily available at stores that sell fabric for dressmaking, sewing, and crafts. It is made of nylon, is extremely lightweight, and doesn't stretch, making it optimal for art quilts that will hang on a wall. The petticoat netting forms the bottom layer of the quilt top to which I pin and then stitch all appliqué pieces and any background pieces. This netting also allows me to sew pieces of the quilt separately and then insert them onto the background fabric, under or over another piece, while still keeping the quilt lightweight. This feature is particularly useful for the quilts in this book that are made from patterns with subpatterns, such as the trees in *Tuscan Sunset* (page 50, patterns pages 61 and 62). Simply make each pattern on its own stabilizer, and then merge the subpattern shapes with the larger pattern.

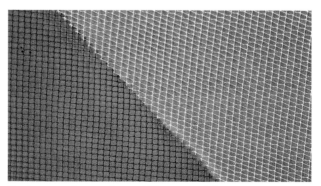

Petticoat netting used as stabilizer material

ACTIVITY 1: Organizing *Your* Stash

You are ready to begin the first activity in preparation for your journey—organizing your tone-on-tone fabrics. Doing this helps refine your understanding of value and also shows you what's missing or in short supply in your stash. Generally the missing values are those in either the very lightest or the darkest ranges.

SUPPLIES

Your tone-on-tone
fabric collection

Eight-Value Gray
Scale (page 34)

Rough sort

Roughly sort all your tone-on-tone fabrics by color into eight piles—red, orange, yellow, green, blue, violet, gray, and black-and-white. Set aside any plaids, calicos, scenics, novelty prints, and other distinctive prints to be stored separately.

NOTE *Where you group a fabric is up to you. This orange-red could go with either the reds or the oranges depending upon your stash.*

Sorting by value

Once your tone-on-tone fabrics are separated into eight color families, it's time to start determining their values—lightness or darkness. The sorting process produces long lines of fabric arranged from very light to dark. Don't worry—you won't need to keep them in these lines once you divide them into values within each color family.

Start by writing the value numbers (Value 1 through Value 8) on eight slips of paper or sticky notes. Now select a color family. If you have a good selection of fabrics, I recommend starting with gray because it's the easiest to read. Gray lacks intensity, color, and temperature (cool and warm colors). If you don't have a good gray stash, start with any color for which you do have a good assortment of values.

Blue stash ready for sorting

Fabrics that range from 1 to 3 on the value scale are tints, *which are noticeably lighter than the 4 and 5, or* midrange, *values. Shades* range from 6 to 8 and appear darker than the midrange fabrics. *Toned (grayed) fabrics will be arranged within colors according to their individual values (lightness or darkness).* TIP

1. Sort the fabrics of a single color family into 3 piles—light, medium, and dark.

2. Starting with the light pile, make a line of fabrics arranged from lightest to darkest.

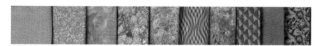

3. Repeat Step 2 with the medium pile.

4. Sort the dark pile, again arranging from lightest to darkest.

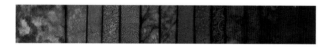

The three blue piles have been sorted from lightest to darkest.

Your stash may not include all eight values in every color. This is not earth shattering! It's typical to have many midrange values but be missing the lightest tints and the darkest shades. Fabric manufacturers tend to produce more midrange values than the lightest and darkest ones. If you find a hole in your stash, see if you can fill it the next time you shop, or you and a friend may want to exchanges pieces.

TIP

Once you have three sorted lines for one color family, examine your lightest line in comparison to the Eight-Value Gray Scale (page 34).

Focus first on the scale's Value 1 gray. Do any of the lightest fabrics in your line come close to it in value? You may have to place the scale directly on the fabric and stand back 3–6 feet to get an accurate reading. Squinting also may help!

Where the fabric and the scale blend best is a fabric's value number. You may or may not have Value 1 fabric(s). If you have a Value 1 fabric, continue sliding the scale along until the Value 1 gray on the scale is *lighter* than the fabric you're holding it against. Place the Value 2 label between that piece and the last fabric that matches the Value 1 gray. This is the beginning of your Value 2 pile. If you do not have a Value 1 fabric, start labeling your stash at the appropriate value on the gray scale. You may have to start at 2, 3, or some other value, depending on the fabrics and the size of your stash.

Superimpose the Eight-Value Gray Scale. The Value 2 label for this line should go between the eleventh and thirteenth fabrics from the left end. This is where the Value 2 grouping ends and the Value 3 fabrics begin.

Repeat this value-sorting exercise with the other two lines of fabric in the color family. Your medium-value fabrics will be sorted into Value 4 and Value 5 groupings, and the dark fabrics will be grouped as Values 6, 7, and 8.

> # NOTE
> *When you are working with Values 6, 7, and 8 in warm colors (red, orange, yellow), red may appear more maroon or burgundy, orange could be a rusty orange or orange-brown, and yellow may be olive green to brown.*

When you have completed your sort, you should have three long lines of fabric, going from the lightest value to the darkest. Now go through the same process for the rest of your color groupings. If you're fortunate, you may have all eight values for all the colors. But most quilters don't. Yea! Fabric shopping time!

Stand back and look at your sorted fabrics. The transition between values should be smooth but noticeable. Still, you will have a range within each value. You can double-check your fabric placement against the Periodic Table of Value in Color (page 33).

Even within a single value, there will be some variation.

Although there is some variance within each eight-value stack, the biggest differences are between values.

Sorting "problem" fabrics

You will probably come across a fabric that you don't quite know where to place. Maybe it's on the dark side of one value and the light side of another, or perhaps it is a toned (muddied or grayed) fabric. There are several ways to decide where it should go. The easiest approach is simply to place the "problem" piece on fabrics of different values to see if you can tell where it belongs.

The arrow indicates the red fabric that needs to be placed.

If you are having real trouble deciding where certain fabrics should be placed within a color family (as opposed to which color family they belong to), one of the following ideas may help.

Photo sort

I took a snapshot of a portion of my green stash and printed it on my home printer, first in color and then in black and white. In the color photo, some greens appeared to be close, or the same in value, while some of the toned greens didn't seem to belong where they were placed. The second picture, printed in black and white, made it easier to compare the toned greens with the others.

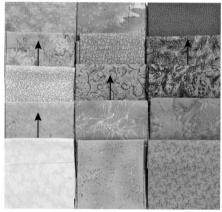

The arrows indicate toned greens I had trouble placing.

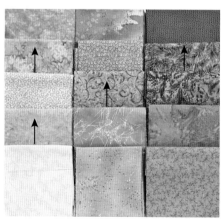

A black-and-white photo helps verify placement of the toned greens.

Scanner/copier sort

This technique is similar to the photo sort, but you use your home copier or scanner to convert your fabrics to black and white.

1. Place several different pieces of fabric *in the same color family* on the glass top of your printer/scanner.

2. Copy, using your printer's black-and-white option. This will give you a sheet of various gray tones.

3. Compare this sheet with the Eight-Value Gray Scale (page 34) or the Periodic Table of Value in Color (page 33).

Caution: This method should only be used to compare colors *within* a color family. The copier sort won't always give an accurate reading when comparing one color with another (yellow with blue, for instance) because some colors are intrinsically more intense than others. Printed in black and white, the more intense colors look lighter, even when they have the same saturation levels as the other colors.

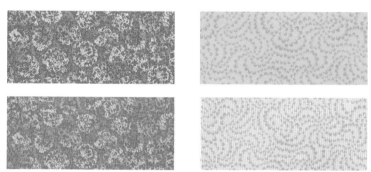

In color, these Value 4 colors appear to be the same value. In black and white or gray scale, the intensity of the yellow makes it appear much lighter.

Beholder sort

A red value finder, sold under the name Ruby Beholder, is a piece of transparent, ruby-colored plastic that translates color into grays when you look through it. A green value finder, or Emerald Beholder, is made of green transparent plastic. You can make your own value finder from transparent red or green cellophane—the kind used to wrap gift baskets. The Ruby Beholder works on any color except red, while the Emerald Beholder works on anything but green.

Arrange your "questionable" fabrics alongside your sorted fabrics where you think they might go. Now look through the value finder. Your fabrics should appear as shades of gray, letting you see just where they should go.

ACTIVITY 2: Making *a* Periodic Table *of* Value in Color

Refer to the Periodic Table of Value in Color (page 33).

Creating your own Periodic Table of Value in Color will give you a visual reference guide for your sewing area; make a smaller version to take on shopping trips or to class. This table and the Color/Value Fan, which you will make in Activity 3 (page 31), are wonderful tools for selecting the fabrics for all the projects in this book—as well as for your own original art designs.

Selecting the fabric

1. Select a color family from Activity 1 (page 23). Start with gray if you have it. Choose a fabric from each of the eight value piles (1 through 8) for that color. Lay out the chosen fabrics on a table in a column, with the lightest value at the top.

NOTE *You don't have to match the hues I used in my large periodic table, just the values. It doesn't matter if the red piece you select for a particular value is blue-red, clear red, or orange-red.*

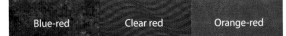

Any of these reds would work for the Value 5 spot on the large periodic table.

---

2. Repeat Step 1 for each color family so that you end up with a column each for gray, red, orange, yellow, green, blue, violet, black/white. As you lay out your fabrics, arrange each color column right next to the previous one, so that you create a grid with the color families going from left to right and the values going

from top to bottom (1 to 8). You may have some gaps if you are missing values in your fabrics.

3. Take a close look to make sure that all the colors going across a given row have the same value. Substitute pieces as necessary. Check the columns for the correct progression of values. When you are satisfied, leave the pieces in place for a couple of days. Take a look occasionally to assess your arrangement and make any further changes.

Cutting the squares

Once you feel that you've made the best choices in value and color, proceed with the following steps:

1. Cut 2 squares 2½″ × 2½″ from each fabric choice (representing all the values for every color family). These squares will be slightly larger than what you actually need, allowing you to overlap seams for a neater-looking board. If you have every value in every color, you should end up with 16 squares for each color family (2 of each value), for a total of 128 squares.

2. One 2½″ square of each fabric cut in Step 1 is for your large periodic table. Cut the matching square into 2 pieces, each 2½″ × 1¼″, for the small periodic table and for the Color/Value Fan in Activity 3 (page 31).

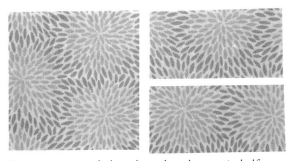

Keep one square whole and cut the other one in half.

3. Cut 2 additional 2½″ × 2½″ squares in black tone-on-tone fabric and 2 more in white tone-on-tone fabric. The white squares will begin and the black squares will end both the gray and the black-and-white columns, creating the table's distinctive "H" shape. These squares illustrate the starting and ending points for the range of values in *all* colors.

What works

Here are some helpful hints for making the periodic table:

- We encountered some problems gluing the pieces to the board. We tried several different types of glue that are safe to use with fabric (acid free and clear drying), and the one that worked best was basting glue (Roxanne's Glue-Baste-It) applied with a needle-nose applicator.

- Don't get carried away with the glue! A thin line or dot along the edges of each grid on the board just prior to applying the appropriate square works best.

- What works even better than gluing is attaching the squares to one side of double-stick fusible webbing. This makes it easy to stick the squares to the board smoothly and evenly and allows for repositioning them prior to pressing.

- A border of very narrow grosgrain ribbon will give the chart a finished appearance and keep the edges from raveling over time.

Important: Do not fuse the fabric squares on foam core board. *The heat of the iron will melt the foam! Use the fusing method only with poster board. Use glue to anchor the fabric squares on foam core board.* TIP

Making the Periodic Table of Value in Color

Use the Periodic Table of Value in Color (page 33) as a reference when placing the fabric squares. With your value-sorted fabric squares at hand (see Cutting the Squares, page 27), you're ready to begin assembling your large table.

SUPPLIES

1 piece white poster board OR 1 piece foam core board, 22″ × 28″

68 quilting squares 2½″ × 2½″ from Cutting the Squares (page 27)

Double-stick fusible webbing (Steam-A-Seam 2, optional) OR fabric glue (Roxanne's Glue-Baste-It)

Pencil

¼″ black grosgrain ribbon for border, at least 3 yards (optional)

Quilting rulers, 6″–12″ and 2½″ square

Rotary cutter and mat

Scissors for fabric and paper

1. Using a pencil (or an eraser if you don't want the lines to show), lightly draw the grid of 2″ squares on your poster or foam core board. This grid will help you align the fabric squares and center the table on the board.

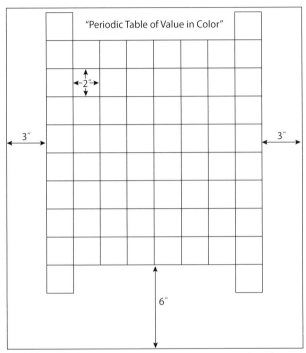

"Periodic Table of Value in Color"

2″

3″   3″

6″

Grid pattern for large periodic table on 22″ × 28″ board

2. Start with the gray fabric if you have it, or red if you don't. **If you are fusing,** place the lightest-value 2½″ square on one side of the fusible webbing and cut it out. Place the square in the correct location on the poster board, with its left side over the left grid line and its top edge over the top grid line, allowing ¼″ to overlap the grid on all sides. Press the squares in place with your hand. Do not iron at this time. **If you are using glue,** lightly apply the glue to the foam core board and position the square as you would for fusing.

3. Working row by row or column by column, fill in the grid. Align the first row or column so that each square overlaps the overhang of the previous one and the outside edges are even. For the remaining rows or columns, align the new fabric squares evenly with the left and top grid lines, placing each new square so that it overlaps the overhang of the previously placed squares. The new squares should extend over the lines on the right and bottom sides. The overlaps will be covered by the next squares or, on the outer edges, by the optional ribbon border. If you are using fusible webbing, once all the pieces are in place and you don't need to reposition any, press with your iron to fuse.

4. If you wish, glue or fuse grosgrain ribbon as a border around the "H" shape of your table.

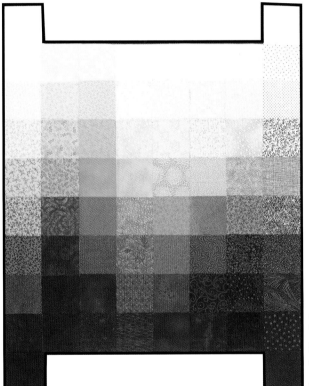

Photo by Dan Snipes

Completed Periodic Table of Value in Color

Making the portable Periodic Table of Value in Color

To create the portable periodic table, fold a full-size white poster board in half so that each half is 22″ × 14″. The bottom half of the poster board becomes the periodic table, and the top half becomes a protective cover that folds over the table.

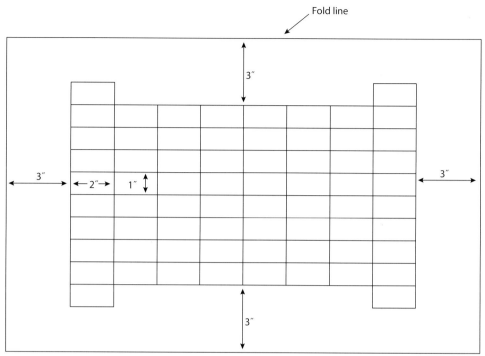

Fold line

3″

3″   ←2″→   1″   3″

3″

Grid pattern for the portable periodic table on the 22″ × 14″ top half of a poster board

To make this table, use the same supplies and repeat Steps 1–4 for the large periodic table (page 29), but this time use the 2½″ × 1½″ fabric pieces. (You'll have pieces left over for the Color/Value Fan, page 31.) Using a pencil, draw a grid of 2″ × 1″ rectangles.

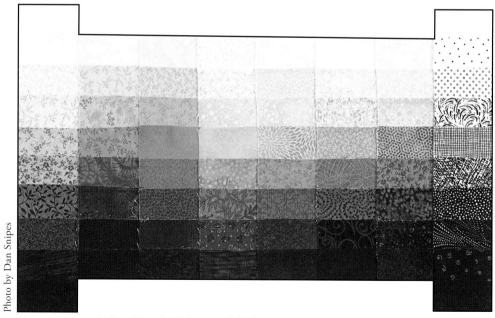

Photo by Dan Snipes

The portable periodic table is half the size of the large version.

IMPRESSIONIST APPLIQUÉ

ACTIVITY 3: Making *a* Color/Value Fan

This tool is a favorite with all of my students. Small enough to take along in your purse or pocket, it is invaluable for choosing fabric of the right value when you go shopping or are simply looking for pieces in your own stash.

Creating the Color/Value Fan

1. Cut 10 strips 2½″ × 10″ from the white poster board. Set the strips aside.

2. Start with Value 1 in the color family of your choice. If you are gluing, skip to Step 3. If you are fusing, place a 2½″ × 1½″ fabric rectangle on the double-stick fusible webbing. Cut out along the edges of the rectangle.

3. Pencil a line across the short side of a 2½″ × 10″ strip of poster board, 1″ from the top. Position the webbing-backed Value 1 rectangle so that its top long edge is aligned with the pencil line; press in place with your hand. Alternatively, glue the fabric rectangle to the poster board strips.

4. If you are gluing, skip to Step 5. Place the Value 2 rectangle on double-stick fusible webbing and cut it out.

5. Measure 1″ down from the top of the Value 1 rectangle and place the top of the Value 2 rectangle along that line. The Value 2 rectangle will overlap the bottom of the Value 1 rectangle by ½″. Press the webbing-backed rectangle in place *with your hand. Do not iron!* Alternatively, glue a nonwebbing-backed fabric rectangle in place with tiny glue beads or a thin line of glue.

6. Repeat Steps 4 and 5 for the remaining fabric rectangles through Value 8, each time measuring down 1″ from the top of the previous rectangle to place the new one. Trim the Value 8 rectangle to 2½″ × 1″ before placement.

7. Flip over the board and trim the strips along the side and bottom edges as needed so that the fabric is flush with the edges of the board. If you are fusing, press with your iron. Trim any loose threads.

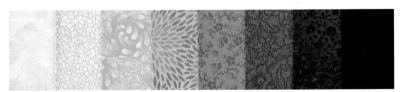

Trimmed eight-value strip

SUPPLIES

The remaining 2½″ × 1½″ value-sorted fabric rectangles from Step 2 of Cutting the Squares (page 27)

1 piece of white poster board, 22″ × 28″

Double-stick fusible webbing OR fabric glue (Roxanne's Glue-Baste-It)

Self-adhesive laminating sheets (optional)

Notebook-paper hole reinforcements

Post and screw, metal key ring, ribbon, or other fastener

Hole punch

Pencil

Quilting rulers, 6″–12″ and 2½″ square

Rotary cutter and mat OR scissors for fabric and paper

8. Repeat Steps 2–7 for each remaining color family. Note that I did not use the all-white or the all-black rectangles on the gray or black-and-white strips.

9. Use the 2 extra poster board strips as back and front covers. Cut the ends of all the strips into arcs—rounded edges are less likely to catch and bend. You can label the blades of your fan, as shown, or leave them plain.

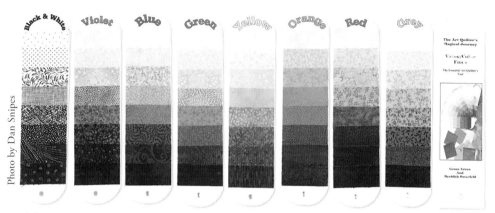

10. If you wish, cover each blade with self-adhesive laminate from an office supply store.

11. Punch a small hole in the bottom end of each blade, lining up the holes. For extra strength, I used notebook-paper reinforcements on each hole. Secure with a ¼″ post and screw from the hardware store or another fastener of your choice.

Your Color/Value Fan is just the right size to take along when you go fabric shopping.

IMPRESSIONIST APPLIQUÉ

For Your Reference

Use these pages as reference guides for sorting your fabrics or putting together your Periodic Table of Value in Color.

Periodic Table of Value in Color

Photo by Dan Snipes

1
2
3
4
5
6
7
8

Eight-Value Gray Scale—paper (left), fabric (right)

Photo by Dan Snipes

MORNING GLORY, 29½" × 27", by Grace Errea

Our first stop along the trail—*Morning Glory*—is a botanical study. This quilt is a remembrance of a beautiful summer morning when I came across a profusion of morning glories tumbling over a low wall near my Southern California home. *Morning Glory* has two major emphases: the use of value to create a focal point and the technique of turned-edge appliqué.

See Essential Supplies (page 20) for additional information.

Foam core board, 40″ × 30″

Straight pins and extra-thin silk pins

Painter's tape

Clear vinyl (such as a painter's drop cloth or a tablecloth, 1–2mm thick), 30″ × 28″ or larger

Black fine-point Sharpie permanent marker

Freezer-paper roll, 18″ wide

Black ballpoint pen

Blue and red erasable pencils

Stabilizer material (petticoat netting), 30″ × 28″ or slightly larger

Scissors for fabric and paper

Craft knife

Stiletto

Spray starch

Cotton swabs

Fabric glue

Clear and smoke-colored nylon thread

Bobbin, prefilled with clear nylon thread **or** 50-weight cotton thread in medium beige and medium gray (if your bobbin won't accept nylon thread)

Embellishments, such as decorative yarn or beads (optional)

Fabric Requirements

Select fat quarters or eighths and lots of smaller scraps for the leaves, flowers, and buds. Your colors can be realistic or fanciful. The pattern's values for all the pieces are based on a Value 1–2 background fabric. Choose a background that doesn't have a distinctive pattern design so that it will set off the flower. Audition several backgrounds with your choice of flower, bud, and leaf fabrics to see what works best. The flower will stand out more prominently if you use medium to dark values for the outer petals.

Rochelle Caffetry auditions fabrics on her background.

If you decide to use something other than a Value 1–2 background, you need to adjust the values of the flower, bud, and leaf fabrics as well. You can't simply substitute the opposite value—a Value 6 with a light background won't necessarily have the same effect as a Value 3 with a dark background. Auditioning fabrics and always keeping a minimum differential of at least three values between the flower and its background are essential.

Leaves: Values 2–7

Flower: Values 5–7 for outer petal portions, Values 1–4 for inner petal portions

Buds: Values 1–7 in the same hue as the flower

Background: Values 1–2, cut 28″ × 24″ or larger

Outer borders (finished 2″-wide top and sides, 3″-wide bottom): Values 7–8, ⅔ yard

Inner border (finished 1″ wide): Values 5–6, ¼ yard

Narrow flange: Value 3, ⅛ yard

Binding: Values 7–8 in the same color as the outer border, ⅓ yard

See A Bouquet of Blossoms (page 48) for inspiration.

Creating *Your* Focal Point

A focal point is an area of interest or emphasis. Refer to Creating a Focal Point (page 15) for various ways a focal point can be created through the use of value. Key points to remember:

- Using differentials of at least two or three values is one of the best ways to create a center of attention.

- Edges need to look clear and sharp against the background.

- Contrasting hues help create an area of interest.

- Contrasting sizes will enhance the focal point. Larger objects (like the blossom) draw more attention when surrounded by smaller ones (the buds and leaves), and vice versa.

- Clear, highly saturated hues (not toned) appear closer to the viewer and are more prominent when surrounded by tinted or shaded hues.

Creating Morning Glory

Morning Glory is created using turned-edge appliqué. With this method, edges that lie on top of other pieces are turned under and appear smooth. As in traditional appliqué quilts, the shapes are placed on the background, starting with the piece that appears farthest from the viewer and ending with the shapes that seem closest. Using pins, rather than fusing or gluing, allows you to move, substitute, and reposition shapes easily at any time prior to stitching. The following sections provide a step-by-step guide to the turned-edge appliqué method as you create your version of *Morning Glory*.

Pattern Notations *and* Instructions

Background V1–2

49 V2 · 48 V4 · 47 V5 · 46 V7 · 45 V4 · 44 V2 · 43 V4 · 42 V3 · 59 V7 · 41 V5 · 14 V2 · 13 V3 · 6 V6 · 5 V6 · 15 V3 · 8 V3 · 7 V4 · 17 V4 · 16 V4 · 1 V7 · 2 V5 · 9 V2 · 12 V1 · 11 V2 · 23 V4 · 40 V4 · 39 V3 · 18 V3 · 20 V5 · 4 V5 · 26 V3 · 19 V4 · 10 V4 · 22 V5 · 38 V4 · 37 V3 · 3 V6 · 21 V6 · 24 V5 · 25 V4 · 34 V5 · 36 V4 · 35 V6 · 55 V6 · 27 V6 · 57 V6 · 56 V6 · 58 V7 · 28 V6 · 33 V7 · 50 V4 · 51 V3 · 32 V6 · 52 V5 · 53 V3 · 31 V7 · 54 V1 · 29 V6 · 30 V7

Background V1–2

Each appliqué piece on the master pattern (pullout page P–1) is outlined with a solid boundary line that serves as the cutting line. The pieces are numbered 1 through 59. Each piece also has a value number, V1 through V8.

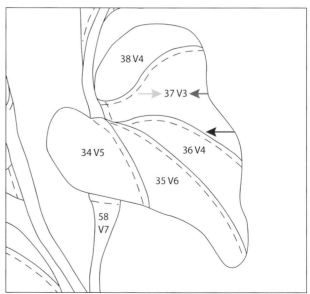

38 V4 · 37 V3 · 34 V5 · 36 V4 · 35 V6 · 58 V7

The red arrow shows the piece boundary/cutting line. The yellow arrow points to the piece number (37), and the blue arrow indicates that this piece should be Value 3.

"Overies" and "Undies"

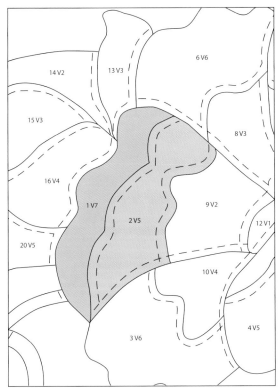

In addition to solid cutting lines, some pattern pieces have dashed lines along some edges. Note the dashed lines in the *blue* section.

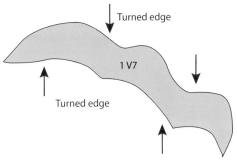

In the *pink* section, all the lines are solid (red arrows), indicating that the edges are turned and will lie on top of another piece in the quilt. These are the "overies."

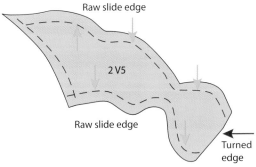

In the *blue* section, dashed lines (yellow arrows) show that three sides will remain raw and will slide under neighboring pieces. These are the "undies." Only the right edge (red arrow) will be turned.

Making *a* Vinyl Overlay

A vinyl overlay will assist you with the correct positioning of the pieces in your quilt top and will serve as a guide for making the freezer-paper templates. The vinyl overlay sits on top of the in-progress quilt top. Simply flip up the overlay, align the next shape you are placing so its outline is in line with the vinyl overlay lines, and then flip the vinyl overlay flat over the quilt top with the new piece pinned in place.

1. Pin the master quilt pattern (pullout page P–1) to your foam core board so it won't slip.

NOTE *If you don't have a foam core board, you can tape the pattern to a flat surface using painter's tape or masking tape. Any light-colored surface will do—a tabletop, the floor—but white works best because it makes it easier to see the lines you are tracing.*

2. Place the clear vinyl over the master quilt pattern and secure it with pins or painter's tape. Make sure the vinyl is larger than the master quilt pattern.

3. Using a fine-tip Sharpie permanent black marker, write your name in a corner of the vinyl overlay to use as a reference. This will help you tell the front from the back when you reverse the vinyl overlay in other steps.

In our experience, Sharpie markers are more permanent than other pens on vinyl. Use a fine tip rather than an ultrafine tip, which has a metal tip guard that can tear the vinyl. TIP

4. With the marker, trace the border of the master quilt pattern on the vinyl overlay. Then trace all the appliqué shapes. Label each appliqué shape with its piece number (1, 2, 3...) and value identification (V1, V2, and so on)

as shown on the master quilt pattern. Dashed lines don't need to be copied onto the vinyl overlay. When finished, you should have a replica of your master quilt pattern on the vinyl overlay *except* for the dashed lines.

5. Remove the master quilt pattern and the vinyl overlay from the foam core board. Roll and store the master quilt pattern for later use in this process.

Photo by Meridith Osterfeld

Making Freezer-Paper Templates

1. Cut 2 sheets of freezer paper the width of your vinyl overlay. Using painter's tape, join the second piece to the first (shiny sides facing the same way) to make a single piece. *Do not use clear cellophane tape*—it will melt when you iron the freezer-paper templates to the fabric! Alternately, join the pieces by overlapping them 1″ and ironing only the overlapped sections (dull side facing up on both sections) to fuse them together.

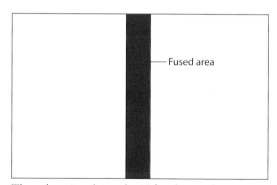

Fused area

The red section shows the 1″ fused area where two sheets of freezer paper overlap (dull side up).

2. Reverse the vinyl overlay so the back is facing you and your name is reversed. Pin the vinyl overlay to the foam core board.

3. Place the joined freezer-paper piece, dull side up, *over* the reversed vinyl overlay. Pin or tape the freezer-paper piece in place.

4. With a black ballpoint pen, trace the quilt pattern border and all the appliqué pieces from the reversed vinyl overlay onto the freezer-paper piece. (It's important to use a ballpoint pen for this and the next step; other pens, including some permanent markers, may run when you wet the fabric with starch solution later in the process.)

> *If you can't see the pattern lines through the freezer paper, tape the reversed vinyl overlay and the freezer-paper piece to a bright window. What you're doing is making the window into a light table. Of course, an actual light table works, too!* TIP

5. When you've finished tracing, write each shape's piece number and value number on the freezer-paper pattern in a normal fashion—that is, not backward as they appear on the reversed vinyl overlay.

6. From the master quilt pattern, copy in *blue* pencil on the freezer-paper pattern the *dashed* lines for edges that *slide* under neighboring pieces. An erasable pencil allows you to change edge notations later, should you need to. Note that the blue dashed lines lie *inside* the appliqué piece that they describe.

7. Use a *red* erasable pencil to outline slightly inside all *solid* black cutting lines, which indicate *turned* edges (they will be turned over on the solid lines of the freezer-paper templates). The fabric is turned over solid edges, and these turned edges will lie on top of—or over—the slide edges. Be sure your red pencil line is *inside* the solid black cutting line; otherwise, you may cut off the edge notation for a particular appliqué template.

> # NOTE
> *Outlining in red lets you know at a glance that this is a turned edge. Red means stop and turn the edge! This notation makes it much easier to keep things straight when an art quilt calls for multiple appliqué techniques (turned edge, raw edge, free edge), as some of the more complex patterns in this book require.*

8. Check that all appliqué shape lines are completely closed. Remove the freezer-paper pattern from the foam core board. Fuse additional pieces of freezer paper to make another large sheet the same size as the previous freezer-paper piece. Use a warm iron to fuse the 2 large sheets together, making sure the shiny (back) side of the freezer-paper pattern faces the dull side of the unmarked sheet. *Your double-thick piece must have a shiny back so you can fuse it to the fabric later.* The doubled freezer-paper template will give you a firm edge for turning the fabric in later steps.

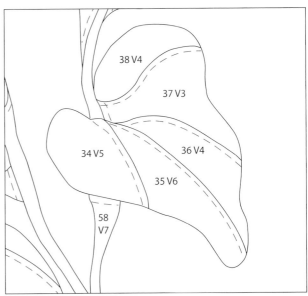

Remember: Blue = dashed = slide edge

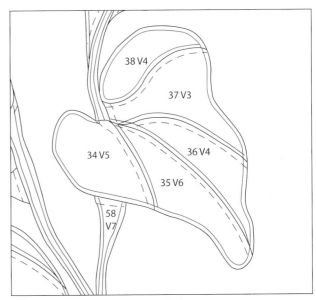

Remember: Red = solid = turned edge

> *You may need to change an edge notation from blue "slide under" to red "turn over," or vice versa, to keep a dark fabric from showing through a lighter one. If a dark outline shows through, try to slide the light fabric under the dark one. If you must place a lighter value on top and a darker value shows through, consider doubling the light fabric piece or line it with white muslin.* TIP

Turned-Edge Appliqué

Preparing Appliqué Pieces

1. Remove the vinyl overlay from the foam core board. Place the stabilizer on the foam core board, and then place the background fabric over the stabilizer. Not all art quilts have a separate background piece.

> NOTE *Depending on the design, you may have to pin and stitch the appliqué shapes directly to the stabilizer to create the background. Or you can create a completely separate pieced background, and then place the foreground on this pieced background.*

2. Place the vinyl overlay *right side up* on top of the stabilizer and background fabric. Pin the vinyl overlay to the foam core board along the top edge only, so you can flip it up when needed.

3. Check that all the edges of each shape on the freezer-paper pattern are marked with a red line or a blue dashed line.

4. Starting with Piece 20 in the left leaf, cut out the freezer-paper template on the solid black cutting line.

> *Cut and work with only one freezer-paper template at a time to minimize confusion and avoid misplacing pieces. If pieces are difficult to reach or to cut accurately with scissors, use a craft or mat knife and a cutting mat. Store your freezer-paper pattern templates in an envelope once you are done with them.* TIP

5. Following the value notation on the piece (V5), select a piece of fabric with this value in your chosen hue. Take it to your pressing area, along with a stiletto, spray starch, small sharp scissors, cotton swabs, and the freezer-paper template.

6. Press the freezer-paper template to the *back* of the fabric. Cut around it, leaving a scant ¼" of fabric extending beyond the turned edges (marked with solid red pencil lines). Leave a healthy ¼"–½" on the raw edges that will slide under another piece (marked with the dashed blue pencil lines).

> NOTE *Leave ½"–1" of fabric on edges that will extend into the area to be bordered or bound. Extra fabric on the edges will prevent gaps that might let the background fabric show through where it isn't supposed to show.*

7. Once you have the fabric with the ironed-on freezer-paper pattern cut out, look at the curves. Concave fabric edges that need to be turned over must be clipped in order to turn them smoothly. Concave is cavelike (curving in), and convex is hill-like (curving out).

Use small, sharp scissors to clip at regular intervals to within a thread or 2 of the edge of the freezer-paper template on any concave areas that will be turned. Take care not to cut all the way to the edge of the paper, or you won't have a smooth edge when you turn the fabric.

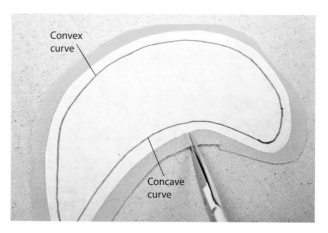

Convex curve

Concave curve

> *The sharper the concave curve, the more cuts you will need to make in order for the edge to turn smoothly. Do not clip convex pieces or edges that will slide under another shape.* TIP

8. Spray a small amount of starch into a container. Moisten a cotton swab with the starch and apply it to the fabric along the edges that will be turned over. Let the starch soak into the fabric for a few seconds; otherwise, flakes like dandruff will form when you press the piece.

9. Using the point of a stiletto and the tip of the iron, turn the fabric a little bit at a time. Hold the turned section in place with the stiletto and apply the hot iron tip, pressing the fabric over the edge of the paper pattern. Work slowly and in very small sections (⅛"–¼" at a time) to achieve the smoothest edge possible. There should be no folds in the fabric.

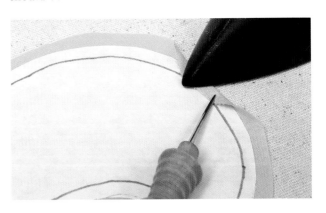

> # NOTE
> *When pressing a turned edge, use an iron that has a sharp point and a thin sole plate (generally the inexpensive models at chain stores). Set the temperature to cotton or linen (hot) on the dry setting (no steam).*

> *In order not to end up with tiny pleats on the convex (hill) portions of curves, you must proceed very slowly and pull the fabric slightly down and away from the oncoming tip of the iron. If you accidentally create a fold, simply wet it with starch and re-iron.*
> # TIP

---

10. If you come to a sharp point on the freezer-paper template, follow Steps 11–13. Otherwise skip to Step 14.

11. Sharp, pointy template tips are turned in stages. Start by pressing the top of the tip inward.

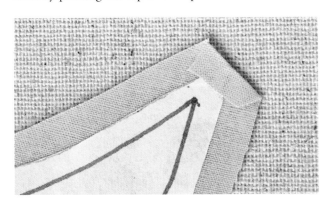

12. Press one side over the tip that you have just pressed in.

13. Continue turning the edge, working your way around the shape until you get to the other side of the point. Press it over what you have already turned, always hugging the freezer-paper template.

14. Once the entire edge is turned and ironed, remove the freezer-paper template. Press the edge again so it is crisp and smooth. Fabric has "memory," so taking out the pattern won't damage the crease if the starch has been ironed thoroughly dry and the crease is sharp.

If you have a very sharp point on a turned-edge piece, place a tiny drop of Roxanne's Glue-Baste-It under the fabric fold. Hold the point in place with your finger until it is dry. TIP

Small bead of glue applied here.

15. Cut off the point's dog-ear so it is flush with the creased edge, angling your scissors under the turned edge as you cut.

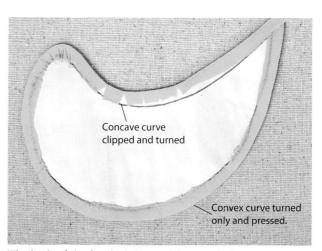

Concave curve clipped and turned

Convex curve turned only and pressed.

The back of the finished shape with turned edges

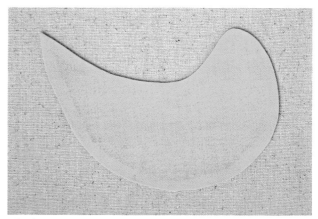

The front of the finished shape with turned edges

16. Use Steps 1-15 as needed to complete each appliqué piece before pinning it in place on the background.

Placing the Appliqué Pieces

Place your first appliqué piece on the background fabric, positioning it under its outline on the vinyl overlay. Raw edges will extend beyond the lines on the vinyl but will eventually be covered by other pieces. Hold the shape in place with one or two silk pins, depending upon the size of the piece. Continue with the rest of the pieces.

TIPS

- *I suggest that you start with Piece 20 (see Preparing Appliqué Pieces, page 42), but it is your choice. When the first piece is in place, work on a neighboring piece; establish a routine of placing a piece, selecting a neighboring piece, and placing the "over" edges over the previous slide edge. Let the new slide edge "run wild," and then cover it with its neighbor. It is not critical which piece goes next, but most quilters do the flower and then the outer leaves, and so on.*

- *To secure a quilt piece under the vinyl overlay, place pins parallel to the edges of the foam core board near the center of the shape. This keeps the edges loose so that other pieces can slide under or over as needed. Pin only through the background fabric and stabilizer, not through the board.*

- *Stems don't have to be cut on the bias. When a complex twist in a stem occurs, you can divide and conquer by cutting it in sections. You don't need to turn under the ends of each stem section; simply butt them or overlap slightly.*

Photo by Meridith Osterfeld

Divide the twisted portion of the stem into three sections to be cut and turned independently. Pin to the quilt top following the vinyl overlay.

Viewing your quilt top

Wait until you have most of the pieces pinned in place before you look at your quilt top without the vinyl overlay. Until then, view it often through the vinyl overlay, looking for any color and value discrepancies. Position the board upright for viewing so the picture isn't distorted, and stand at least 6–10 feet away.

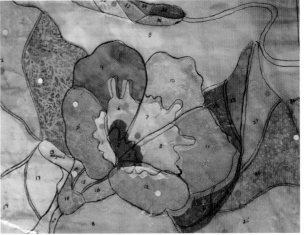

Photo by Meridith Osterfeld

Pins with large glass or flower heads can keep you from seeing the image as a whole.

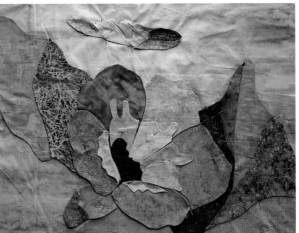

Photo by Meridith Osterfeld

Fasten the pieces with plain silk pins so you can view your quilt without distraction.

When the quilt top is almost complete, flip the vinyl overlay to the back and prop up the board. Move 6 or more feet away to get a really good view of your creation. If the space you are working in doesn't allow you to get far enough away, try looking at the quilt in a mirror.

Stitching

On top use clear nylon thread for pieces in the light value range (V1–V5) and smoke-colored nylon thread for pieces in the dark value range (V6–V8). The key is to match the thread's value to that of the appliqué piece, *not* to the background. Always use clear nylon thread in the bobbin. If you have a machine that doesn't accept nylon bobbin thread, substitute 50-weight cotton thread in medium beige for light fabrics and medium gray for darker fabrics. The dark thread in the pictures at right was used for illustration purposes only.

1. Prepare your quilt top by pinning the shapes to the background fabric and stabilizer with silk pins every 1″ to 1½″. Position the pins so that the thin tips face out at a right angle to the edge and the heads face in; this will allow you to sew over the pins.

2. Use an open-toe (embroidery) foot and select the blind hem stitch. With this stitch, the needle sews straight for a few stitches and then jumps over, or "zigs," to stitch the fabric to the left or right of the straight sewing line. If you don't have a blind hem stitch, use the zigzag stitch.

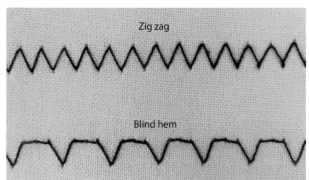

Zig zag

Blind hem

Photo by Meridith Osterfeld

3. Adjust the machine so the stitch sews about ⅛″ (approximately 3mm) and then "zigs" left or right for a bite of the appliqué fabric. The jump onto the shape should be just enough to catch 1 or 2 threads.

Only a couple of threads should be caught in the "zig" onto the appliqué shape.

4. Starting at one edge of the quilt top, stitch around all the edges of the light-value appliqué pieces with clear thread. Then change to smoke thread for the top thread and stitch the dark-value appliqué pieces. This way, you need fewer changes of thread. Remember that the bobbin thread is always clear or medium neutral.

Use this same approach for all your turned-edge art quilts.

Stitching curves

The needle must be extended down into the background fabric for you to smoothly navigate curves. With the needle down so that it anchors the fabric, raise the presser foot and turn the quilt top as needed to hug the curve with the stitching line. Lower the presser foot and resume stitching.

Stitching points

As you get close to a point, count stitches to ensure that your needle will be on the appliqué shape (the "zig" in the blind hem stitch) at the tip of the point. If you think you will overshoot the tip, gently hold back the fabric to create some resistance.

At the point, keep the needle down in the fabric, raise the presser foot, turn the quilt top in the new stitching direction, lower the foot, and resume sewing.

Stitching deep dips

As you approach a dip in a shape, slow down and make sure that you have a few shorter stitches in the dip to secure the area well. Operate the flywheel manually, if you need to, in order to shorten the stitches. Count stitches and hold the quilt top to create resistance so that you can control where the stitches land.

If points or dips are very sharp, they may need extra stitching for reinforcement. Change the stitch from blind hem to zigzag, sew the area in question, and then revert back to the blind hem stitch.

The Finishing Touches

With all the pieces stitched in place, you may want to add some embellishment to the morning glory blossom. I used small bits of colorful yarn for one version of the quilt and yarn with beadwork for another, but you can choose your own embellishments. If you decide to use yarn, insert it under Piece 11 in the center of the flower *before* you stitch that shape in place.

Add any beading *after* the quilting step (page 91), so the stitching won't damage the beads.

For suggestions on how to convert your quilt top into a magical textile art piece, turn to Celebrating Your Journey (page 87). As shown, *Morning Glory* has a double border with a three-dimensional accent piece, or flange, inserted between the two borders. The fabric requirements given for the quilt include these edge pieces.

Yarn makes a decorative center for this morning glory.

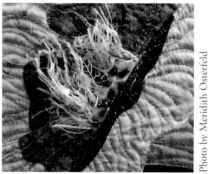

Beadwork was added to this blossom after it was quilted.

After completing the quilt top but before adding the borders, press, square up, and trim the quilt top to 23½″ × 20″. Cut the inner border pieces 1½″ wide so they finish 1″ wide. Cut the flange 1″ wide and fold it lengthwise, wrong sides together (see Note, pagae 88). Stitch the flange to the inner border with raw edges aligned using a ¼″ seam allowance. Cut the outer border pieces for the top and sides 2½″ wide and the bottom outer border piece 3½″ wide. After the borders are in place, block and square up the quilt top to 29½″ × 27″. For more on blocking and squaring your quilt, see Finishing Touches, page 93.

A Bouquet *of* Blossoms

Samples of student work demonstrate that the palette for *Morning Glory* can be interpreted in a number of different ways.

Made by Rochelle Cafferty

Made by Janice Ely

Made by Sondra Gray

Made by Debra Scarlata

Photo by Meridith Osterfeld

Photo by Meridith Osterfeld

Photos by Meridith Osterfeld

For Further Inspiration

Photo by Dan Snipes

GLORIOUS MORNING, 52" × 56", by Grace Errea

Glorious Morning uses multiple morning glory blossoms, buds, and leaves, providing an excellent example of the use of value to create multiple focal points. The same turned-edge appliqué technique as used in *Morning Glory* is used here. However, by creating additional blossoms, buds, leaves, and vines, and then arranging them on a pieced background, you can take your experience to a whole new level.

Photo by Meridith Osterfeld

TUSCAN SUNSET, 27" × 20", by Grace Errea

Our second stop along the trail allows you to enjoy the beauty of the land painted by the setting sun. *Tuscan Sunset* emphasizes the role of value in developing the appearance of three dimensions through atmospheric perspective. This project also introduces the technique of raw-edge appliqué with no fusing.

Fabric Requirements

Refer to the pattern pieces on pages 61 and 62 and pullout page P–2.

For the landscape and trees, you need greens, rosy colors, oranges, golds, peaches, and violets. Choose fat quarters and smaller scraps in a variety of tone-on-tone fabrics in the values indicated on the pattern pieces.

continued on next page

SUPPLIES

See Essential Supplies (page 20) for additional information and basic equipment.

Foam core board, 40″ × 30″

Straight pins and extra-thin silk pins

Painter's multiuse tape or masking tape

Clear vinyl (such as a painter's drop cloth or a tablecloth, 1–2mm thick), 29″ × 22″ or larger

Black fine-point Sharpie permanent marker

Freezer-paper roll, 18″ wide

Black ballpoint pen

Blue erasable pencil

Stabilizer material (petticoat netting), 29″ × 22″ or larger

Scissors for fabric and paper

Craft knife

Cotton swabs

Fabric stiffener (such as Fray Block by June Tailor)

Long-handled tweezers

Clear and smoke-colored nylon thread

Bobbin prefilled with clear nylon thread **or** 50-weight cotton thread in medium beige and medium gray (if bobbin doesn't accept nylon thread)

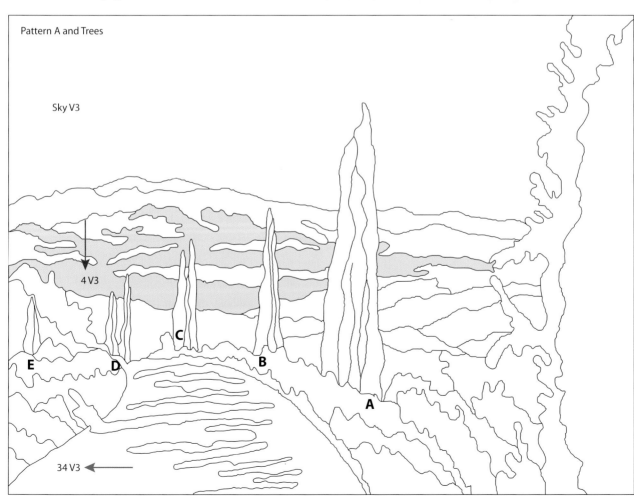

Pattern A and Trees

Sky V3

4 V3

34 V3

A

B

C

D

E

continued from previous page

For the sky, you need a 30″ × 15″ piece of "sunset" fabric in Value 3. Large areas within the landscape—such as Piece 4 (indicated by the red arrow) and the roadway, Piece 34 (blue arrow)—reflect the value of the sky and should also be Value 3. If you use a darker or lighter sky fabric, the value of these large pieces will need to be adjusted.

For the binding, you need ⅓ yard in the color of the sky, value 6–7.

The tree shadows on the roadway, shown in this close-up, are actually a deep violet rather than a shade of black or gray. Don't be afraid to think outside the box about color for shadows—consider dark violets, greens, blues, or browns rather than black or gray.

TIP

Photo by Grace Errea

See A Sunset Sampler (page 59) for further inspiration.

Achieving Dimensionality *through* Atmospheric Perspective

The idea here is to give the quilt a three-dimensional appearance. Using atmospheric perspective is one way of doing this (see Creating a Three-Dimensional Appearance, page 16).

Keep these things in mind when using value to create a three-dimensional art piece:

- Lighter values or toned hues tend to make background objects appear hazy and distant, creating atmospheric perspective. Foreground pieces are generally more saturated with color and should differ in value from background pieces. In this quilt, the road and sky are considered part of the pieced background. The trees and shrubs are in the foreground.

- The composition's purest hues should be used for foreground objects to make them seem closer. They should have crisp, clearly defined edges.

- Warm hues—red, orange, and yellow—in their purest form appear to advance toward the viewer. Cool hues seem to recede.

- Larger objects (like the foreground trees in *Tuscan Sunset*) seem to be closer when juxtaposed with smaller ones (like the shrubs and grasses).

Creating *Tuscan Sunset*

Tuscan Sunset is created using raw-edge appliqué, which means that exposed fabric edges appear to be cut, or "raw." You will follow a traditional appliqué layering method, starting with the pieces that you want to appear the most distant and ending on top with the shapes that you want to appear closest to the viewer.

Pattern Notations *and* Instructions

There are two patterns for *Tuscan Sunset* shown in the illustrations on pages 53 and 54. Pattern A for the sky, bushes, fields, road, and large cypress tree on the right side of the quilt is on pullout page P–2. Pattern B for the remaining cypress trees A–E is at the end of the project (pages 61 and 62). Separating out these trees allows for continuous fabric placement behind the trees, meaning fewer pins and less starting and stopping of stitching.

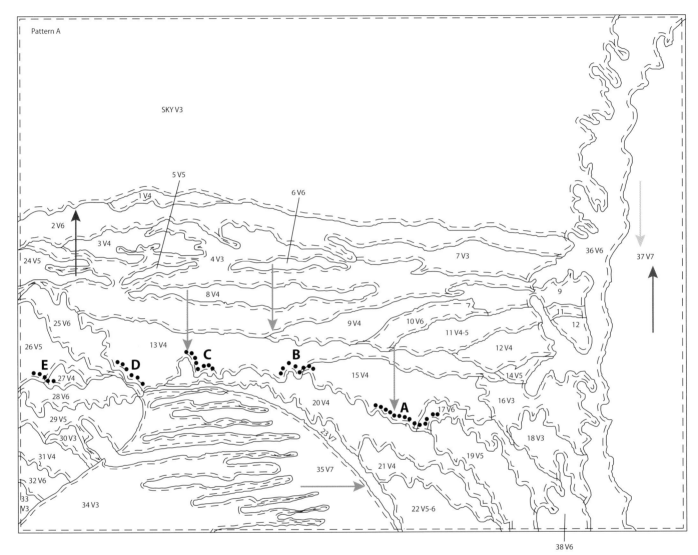

Pattern A (Pieces 1–38)—Solid lines, as indicated by the red arrow, outline each shape and serve as the cutting lines for the freezer-paper templates. Each piece also has a value number (blue arrow) and a piece number (yellow arrow). The patterns also have dashed lines (green arrow), indicating the edges that slide under other pieces. The orange arrows indicate black dots on shapes that will have "pockets" where trees will be inserted prior to stitching.

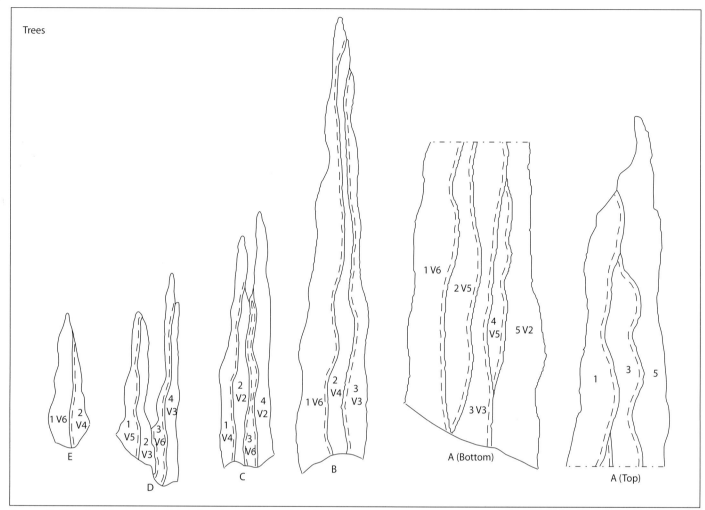

Trees

E   D   C   B   A (Bottom)   A (Top)

Pattern B (Trees)—The trees are labeled A through E. Each individual shape is marked with a piece number and a value number (V1–V8). The patterns are on pages 61 and 62.

Making *the* Vinyl Overlays *and* Templates

Refer to Making a Vinyl Overlay (page 39) and Making Freezer-Paper Templates (page 40) to prepare the vinyl overlays and the freezer-paper templates.

You will prepare one vinyl overlay for the large landscape Pattern A and one for the trees in Pattern B. You will also prepare two freezer-paper patterns—one for Pattern A and one for Pattern B.

1. Prepare a vinyl overlay of the landscape Pattern A. Use a fine-tip Sharpie marker to add the pattern piece numbers, the values, and the black dots indicating where the trees are to be inserted. When finished, you will have a vinyl replica of your master pattern, but without the dashed lines.

2. Using a ballpoint pen, prepare a freezer-paper version of Pattern A. (Reverse the vinyl overlay before you start.) Mark all the slide-under edges with dashed lines in blue pencil. This is important, because these need to be cut differently than the unmarked edges that go on top of other pieces.

3. Remove the freezer-paper pattern from the vinyl overlay.

4. Remove the vinyl overlay and the master quilt pattern. Place the stabilizer on the foam core board; then position the sky fabric over the stabilizer.

5. Place the vinyl overlay, right side up, on top of the stabilizer and the sky fabric. Pin the overlay to the board along the top only, so you can lift the vinyl overlay when needed.

> *Because none of the edges are turned in raw-edge appliqué, there is no need to double the freezer paper for your pattern. Freezer paper is doubled in turned-edge appliqué to make a firm edge for turning the fabric.*
>
> **TIP**

Raw-Edge Appliqué

Preparing Appliqué Pieces

Cut and work with only one template piece at a time to avoid losing pieces and to minimize confusion. Use an envelope to store cut template pieces.

It is important to recognize which edges on a shape go under other pieces and which go over. The "undies" need to have a generous ¼"–½" seam allowance so the stabilizer won't show. The "overies" in raw-edge appliqué get trimmed right up to the edge of the freezer-paper template. You can leave up to 1" allowance on outer edges where you will attach a binding or border.

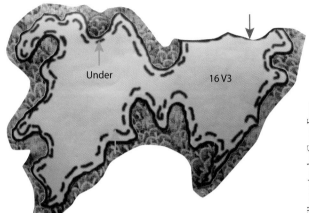

The fabric is trimmed to the solid line on the upper right edge of this piece (red arrow). Dashed lines (green arrow) indicate where the shape will slide under other pieces; these edges need a generous ¼" fabric allowance beyond the template.

Layering the Pieces

In general, layer pieces on the stabilizer from the background to the foreground, with the bottom edges of most pieces covered by the next pieces down. For example, the bottom edge of the sky is under the most distant mountain. By placing the sky first, you can layer the mountains, hills, bushes, and fields over it.

However, there are a few exceptions to this layering procedure: specifically the road, the tree shadows, and the large cypress tree on the right. The road and the shadows are foreground pieces, but they come first because the bush and shrub shapes overlap most of their edges.

The following guides you through the layering process:

1. Once the sky is in place, continue with the road. It is easiest to cut the road (Piece 34) as a continuous solid piece that includes the shadow (Piece 35). Cut on the solid line for the entire shape. Place the shadow over this large piece.

2. Press the shiny side of the template to the back of the fabric you are using for the road. Cut according to the edge instructions.

3. Gently remove the freezer-paper template. If you pull too rapidly, you may end up with loose threads.

> *If you are working with a loosely woven fabric or one that tends to ravel, moisten the edges with a cotton swab dipped in Fray Block or other fabric stiffener before removing the freezer-paper template. This will release the fabric with little or no fraying. Then lightly press the piece with an iron.* **TIP**

4. Place the fabric shape on the stabilizer directly under its outline on the vinyl. The edges that slide under another piece will extend beyond the lines on the vinyl but will be covered later by other pieces. Pin the shape to the stabilizer (not to the board), leaving the edges free.

> *Long-handled tweezers come in handy for positioning fabric shapes on the stabilizer under the vinyl overlay.* **TIP**

5. Cut out the shadow template (Piece 35) from the combined road and shadow template. Press it onto the fabric. Cut the fabric, position it on top of the road under the vinyl overlay, and secure with pins.

6. Cut out and place the pieces for the large cypress tree that forms the complete right side of the quilt top.

7. Starting with Piece 1 and working one shape at a time, cut out and place the remaining pieces, moving from the back toward the foreground of the picture.

Place pieces on the stabilizer under the vinyl overlay.

8. Once all the pieces are secured, mark the pockets (series of dots) where the cypress trees will be "planted," using the vinyl overlay as a guide. Use a water-soluble marker or pins. Leave the dotted line unstitched.

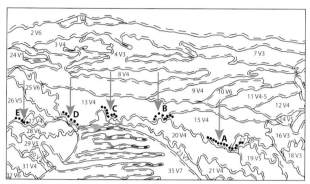

Black dots on the pattern (orange arrows) show where trees will be inserted.

Pins mark the tree insertion points on the quilt top.

> *View your quilt top through the vinyl overlay frequently, looking for any color and value discrepancies. Wait until the quilt top is at least three-quarters complete before you look at it without the vinyl overlay.* **TIP**

9. When the top is complete, leave it up on the board or on a design wall for several days and glance at it often to gain perspective. If something isn't quite how you want it, you can still change it.

IMPRESSIONIST APPLIQUÉ

Stitching Appliqué Pieces

1. Use clear nylon thread on top for all the light-value pieces (V1–V5); switch to smoke-colored nylon thread on top for dark value pieces (V6–V8). Match the thread color to the value of the appliqué piece, not to the background. Use clear nylon bobbin thread for all pieces. If your sewing machine won't accept nylon bobbin thread, use medium beige cotton thread in the bobbin for warm-color fabric pieces and medium gray for cool-color fabric pieces.

2. Attach shapes to the stabilizer every 1″–1½″ with silk pins, with the thinnest part of the pin facing out at right angles to the edge of the shape (so you can sew over the pin). You don't need to pin all the edges at once. Pin just the ones you will be sewing; then stitch, remove the pins, and continue to the next area.

3. Use either an open-toe embroidery foot or a free-motion (darning) foot. Set the stitch length for 10–12 stitches per inch. Starting at one edge of the quilt top, stitch all the light-value areas with clear thread. Then change the top thread and stitch all the dark-value areas with smoke thread. Reminder: For *Tuscan Sunset*, don't stitch the lines where you will insert the trees!

4. Straight stitch each appliqué piece in place, as close to the edge as possible—approximately ¹⁄₁₆″, or 3–4 threads, from the edge. Light-colored cotton thread has been used in the example to make the stitching line clearly visible in the photo.

The embroidery foot has a large opening in front that lets you see exactly where you are sewing.

Using the free-motion foot means you don't have to turn the quilt on every curve.

The bottom piece was stitched with light cotton thread to show up in the photo; the middle piece was stitched with clear nylon thread, which you would actually use for your quilt top.

Adding the Trees

1. Join the top and bottom portions of the pattern template for Tree A. Following the same steps that you used for landscape Pattern A (page 54), create a vinyl overlay and a freezer-paper pattern for each tree (A–E).

2. Make and cut a freezer-paper pattern for each tree using one shape for each. Mark each piece with a letter and value number and add the edge notations. Cut out the templates.

3. Pin the stabilizer and the vinyl overlay to an empty portion of the foam core board.

4. Cut out the tree pieces and pin them to the stabilizer, assembling each tree according to the vinyl overlay. (The trees are cut out individually, so you don't need to arrange them on the stabilizer the same way they are pictured here.)

5. Stitch each tree through the stabilizer, sewing only the interior seams. *Do not stitch the outside edges of the trees.*

6. Cut away the stabilizer so that its edges fall ¹⁄₁₆″–⅛″ inside the fabric edges (white arrows).

7. Locate the marked tree pockets in the background shrub pieces and insert the trees as marked on the vinyl overlay. Stitch the trees in place along the tree bases and outside edges only.

The Finishing Touches

Once you have finished stitching the quilt top, decide whether you want to border your quilt or simply bind the raw edges as I did. Turn to Celebrating Your Journey (page 87) for pointers on edge treatments. After blocking, I squared off and trimmed my quilted top to 27″ × 20″. For more on blocking and squaring, see Finishing Touches, page 93.

A Sunset Sampler

Here are some of the ways students have interpreted *Tuscan Sunset*. As you can see, there is no single "right" color palette for this project. The quilt you create will be an expression of your own artistic vision.

Made by Kar Hoffman

Made by Lynn Fortner

Made by Monika Schurter

Made by Susan Sall

Made by Jean Impey

Made by Pat Bankston

For Further Inspiration

Photo by Dan Snipes

RAINBOW CANYON, 44" × 60", by Grace Errea

What might have been a ho-hum landscape has been transformed through the magic of value and color. *Rainbow Canyon* was created using raw-edge appliqué.

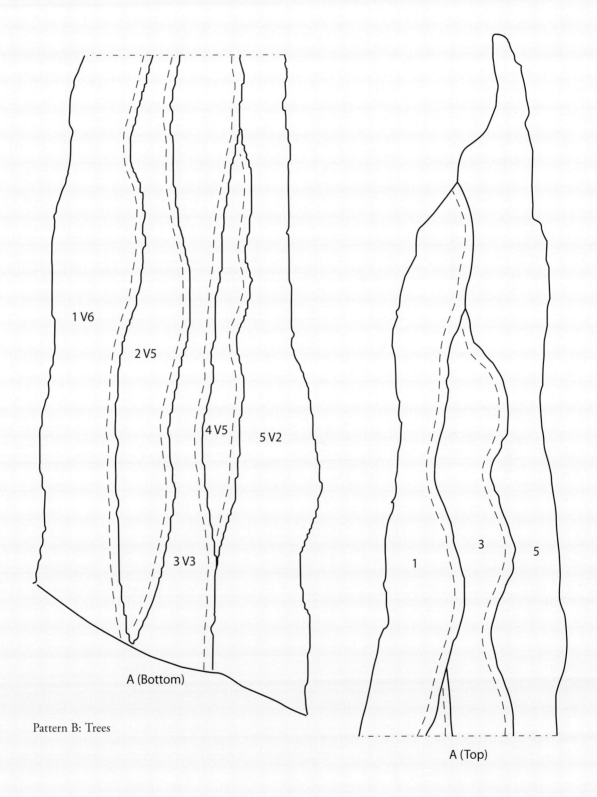

1 V6

2 V5

4 V5

5 V2

3 V3

A (Bottom)

Pattern B: Trees

1

3

5

A (Top)

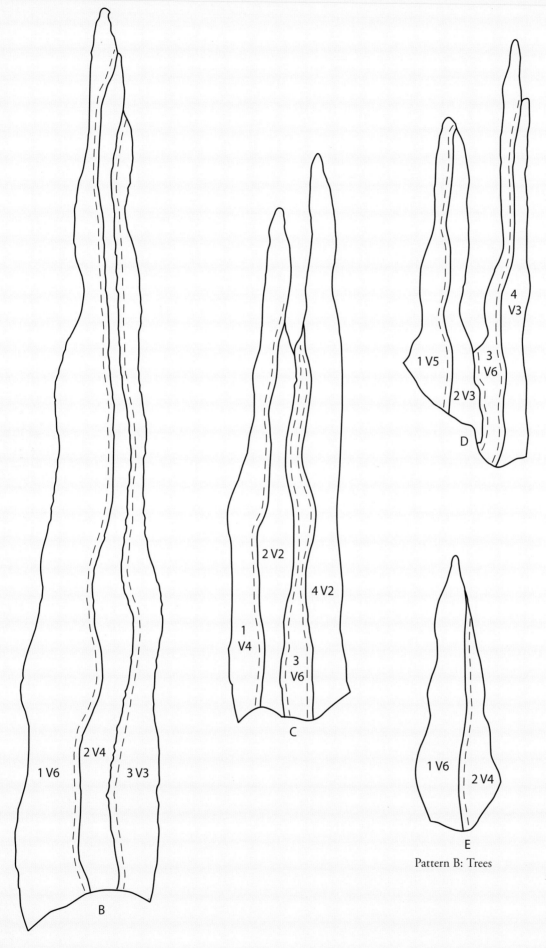

1 V5

4
V3

3
V6

2 V3

D

2 V2

4 V2

1
V4

3
V6

C

2 V4

1 V6   3 V3

B

1 V6

2 V4

E

Pattern B: Trees

IMPRESSIONIST APPLIQUÉ

Photo by Dan Snipes

THE EAGLE, 28½" × 20", by Grace Errea

The next stop on our journey gives us a chance to admire one of our local inhabitants—the American bald eagle. With *The Eagle*, we pay tribute to our national emblem while strengthening our understanding of using value to create the appearance of three dimensions.

This project also introduces the third of our appliqué techniques—free-edge appliqué. *The Eagle* illustrates the use of both raw-edge and free-edge appliqué in a single project and the use of water-soluble thread for basting.

Foam core board, 40″ × 30″

Straight pins and 1″–1½″ extra-thin silk pins

Painter's multiuse tape or masking tape

Clear vinyl (such as a painter's drop cloth or a tablecloth, 1mm–2mm thick), 30″ × 22″ or larger

Black fine-point Sharpie permanent marker

Freezer-paper roll, 18″ wide

Black ballpoint pen

Blue erasable pencil

Stabilizer material (petticoat netting), 22″ × 30″ or larger

Water-soluble basting thread

Nylon thread in clear and smoke color

Bobbin prefill with clear nylon thread **or** 50-weight cotton thread in neutral colors (if bobbin doesn't accept nylon thread)

Fabric Requirements

Refer to the pattern on pullout page P–3 and the feather patterns on page 72.

Use fat quarters and smaller scraps for this quilt. The values and color choices for the eagle's face were designed to work with either light or dark feathers. Staying true to the toned yellow specified for the beak and eye area lets you play with the feather area in different colors and values. A toned yellow was chosen because the large beak and eyes tend to draw the viewer's eye; very bright or unusual colors may overwhelm your feather choices.

- Beak and eyes—Use Values 2–3 in yellow; use Values 4–7 in ochre (toned yellow-brown) and browns for the beak and in off-white, light orange, medium yellow, and black for the eyes.

- Feathers—You'll want a large assortment in at least four different values. You can make the feathers different values of a single color, use multiple colors, or choose different colors for different quadrants of the eagle.

Note: Since there is no background fabric, you need many feathers to adequately cover the stabilizer. To reduce the number of feathers you have to cut, set aside some larger pieces of fabric in the middle range of the colors you have chosen. For instance, if you selected tints in the Value 1–4 range, you'll want fabric pieces of the same color in the Value 2–3 range. If you chose shades in the Value 5–8 range, you'll want Value 6–7 pieces of the same color. These are placed over the stabilizer like a background—the skin on a bird—so that you don't need as many feathers.

- Throat—Under the beak use scraps of a darker value to go with the colors you chose for the throat feathers to create a shadow effect.

- Binding—⅓ yard of fabric in the value and hue of your choice to coordinate with the feathers. Pick a darker value of a hue present in the eagle's feathers.

See Birds of a Feather (page 70) for inspiration.

> *Many gray fabrics have a definite cast of green, violet, or another color. The gray used for* The Eagle *has a violet cast.* TIP

Eagle Beak and Eye Value and Colors

Piece	Value	Color	Piece	Value	Color	Piece	Value	Color
1	1	Off-white	21	6	Violet	41	4	Yellow/Ochre
2	3	Yellow	22	7	Violet	42	5	Yellow/Ochre
3	2	Yellow	23	6	Yellow/Ochre	43	7	Violet
4	3	Yellow	24	6	Gray	44	6	Violet
5	3	Yellow	25	2	Gray	45	5	Yellow/Ochre
6	4	Yellow/Ochre	26	7	Violet	46	4	Gray
7	4	Yellow/Ochre	27	2	Gray	47	3	Gray
8	7	Brown/Yellow/Ochre	28	3	Gray	48	5	Gray
9	6	Brown/Yellow/Ochre	29	4	Gray	49	2	Gray
10	5	Yellow/Ochre	30	4	Orange	50	3	Gray
11	7	Brown/Yellow/Ochre	31	Bl**	Black	51	4	Gray
12	7	Brown/Yellow/Ochre	32	Wh*	White	52	3	Yellow
13	7	Brown/Yellow/Ochre	33	3	Orange	53	Bl**	Black
14	7	Brown/Yellow/Ochre	34	Bl**	Black	54	7	Violet
15	4	Yellow/Ochre	35	3	Yellow	55	4	Orange
16	5	Yellow/Ochre	36	2	Gray	56	3	Orange
17	6	Yellow/Ochre	37	3	Gray	57	Bl**	Black
18	4	Yellow/Ochre	38	2	Gray	58	Wh*	White
19	6	Yellow/Ochre	39	3	Yellow	59	2	Gray
20	5	Yellow/Ochre	40	6	Yellow/Ochre	60	7–8	Red/Orange

*Wh specifies white.   ** Bl specifies black.*

The Magic *of* Light *and* Shadows

Light and shadow help create an illusion of proximity and depth. Following are some key points to remember to give *The Eagle* a three-dimensional appearance:

- Value gives the eagle's facial features—particularly the beak—a sense of volume, creating dimension. The light areas in the center of the beak appear closest to the viewer. Moving away from the center, the beak gradually darkens in value and appears to recede.

- The difference in value between the feathers and the outer edges of the beak makes the beak seem closer to the viewer. The addition of the thin black line to delineate the mouth distinguishes the beak from the feathers. The beak and eyes are the largest pieces and have the cleanest edges, giving the viewer the sense of greatest proximity.

- Off-white and yellow hues in the beak and eyes catch the viewer's eye first because of their intensity.

Creating *The Eagle with* Free-Edge Appliqué

The eagle's beak and eyes are created using raw-edge appliqué, the same as for *Tuscan Sunset* (page 50). The feathers are created using free-edge appliqué. In this technique, all exposed edges are left raw and unattached, or "free," giving them the appearance of real feathers. The background is covered with overlapping layers of feathers, basted with water-soluble thread to temporarily hold them in place. In the final steps, the face and the centers of the feathers are quilted.

Beak and Eyes

Pattern Instructions *and* Guide Notations

There are two major patterns for *The Eagle*. Pattern A for the mouth, beak, and eyes is on pullout page P–3. Pattern B for the feathers is on page 72. Two additional placement guides are included in this project: The mouth guide (page 73) shows how to place the fabric piece for the thin dark line (page 68) that provides visual separation between the upper and lower beak. The feather guide (page 73) indicates where to insert the feathers and how to angle them.

Face of the Eagle

The mouth, beak, and eyes are constructed first. Once the face is pinned in place, the feathers are placed under and around it. We do it in this order for two reasons: First, once you see the eyes staring at you, it becomes difficult to leave the quilt unfinished! Second, you'll be able to discern the most appropriate arrangement of the feather values and colors more clearly once the face is in place.

The pattern pieces for the mouth, beak, and eyes are numbered 1–60. Solid black lines are the cutting lines and indicate edges that will lie *over* another piece. Dashed lines indicate edges that will slide *under*. If you want an eagle that is similar to the one pictured, the Eagle Beak and Eye Value and Colors table (page 65) indicates the piece numbers, values, and colors to use for the beak and eyes.

Creating *the* Quilt Top

The steps for creating the vinyl guides and templates for *The Eagle* are the same as for *Tuscan Sunset* (see Making a Vinyl Overlay, page 39, and Making Freezer-Paper Templates, page 40) because the entire face is done in raw-edge appliqué (see Raw-Edge Appliqué, page 55). The only exception is the mouth (Piece 60), for which special directions have been provided.

1. Trace the mouth, beak, and eyes (Pattern A) onto the vinyl overlay. You don't need to make a vinyl guide for the feathers.

> NOTE *Remember—you do not need to mark the dashed lines on the vinyl overlay, only on the freezer-paper templates.*

2. Reverse the vinyl overlay. Using a ballpoint pen, trace the vinyl overlay to make the freezer-paper pattern.

3. Mark all the freezer-paper shapes with their piece numbers (1–60). Use the Eagle Beak and Eye Value and Colors table (page 65) to mark the appropriate values on each piece.

4. Remove the vinyl overlay. Using blue erasable pencil, mark the dashed lines from the master quilt pattern onto the freezer-paper pattern.

The Mouth, Beak, and Eyes

Position the stabilizer on the board. Pin the mouth, beak, and eyes vinyl overlay, right side up, on the board so the eagle's face is centered on the stabilizer. Pin the vinyl overlay along the top edge so you can flip it up as needed.

In *The Eagle*, you will notice a thin line where the upper and lower portions of the beak meet. This line (Piece 60) is the first shape that you will place, because it consists entirely of "undie" edges except for the very tip of the beak. Because the piece is so narrow, the dashed lines are not shown. Instead, the mouth guide (page 73) gives instructions for cutting Piece 60.

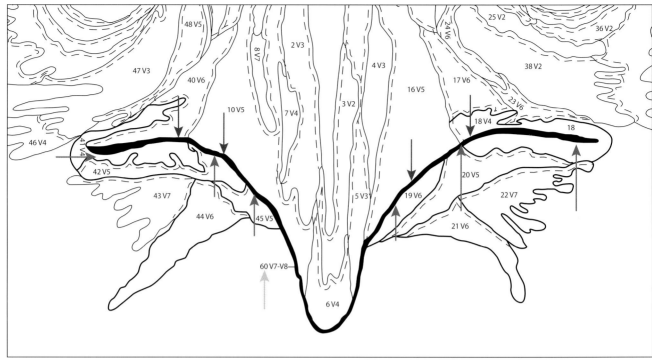

Beak close-up, showing which pieces Piece 60 lies under and which pieces it goes over

At the top, mouth area pieces (red arrows) are separated by Piece 60 from the bottom mouth pieces (blue arrows). Piece 60, indicated by the yellow arrow, fits between all of these pieces and is under them. At the tip of the beak, Piece 60 will have feathers stuffed under it.

1. Using a craft knife and a cutting mat, cut Piece 60 from the freezer-paper pattern along the black solid line.

> *Some students found it easier to reverse the vinyl overlay and trace the skinny mouth shape onto a separate piece of freezer paper rather than cut it out of the large freezer-paper pattern.* TIP

2. Use an iron to press the freezer-paper template to the back of the mouth fabric. Cut out the fabric, using the solid green line shown on the guide (page 73) as your cutting line. The green line shows how much seam allowance you need all around the template.

3. Pin the mouth piece to the stabilizer, using the vinyl overlay as a positioning guide.

4. Continue placing all the other pieces, one at a time, for the beak and eyes, following the raw-edge appliqué technique (no turned edges).

5. Make sure each piece is pinned securely in place. Leave the outside border edges unpinned so that you can insert feathers under them.

Feather Patterns and Guide

The feather patterns (page 72) and the feather guide (page 73) work together. The patterns show you how to make the feathers, while the guide shows the correct direction to angle them away from the beak and eyes.

1. Copy the feather patterns onto freezer paper *without* reversing the vinyl overlay. (Position them on the freezer paper however you want.) Label the feather templates top, bottom and side.

2. Start in one area and choose 6–8 fabrics with a range of 3 or 4 values, such as 1–4, 3–6, and so on.

Stack the fabric, right sides up. Decide whether you will cut right-facing feathers or left-facing feathers.

- **For right-facing feathers**, leave the fabric stack right side up. Iron the freezer-paper template to the front side of the top fabric in the stack.

- **For left-facing feathers**, turn the fabric stack upside down so the back of the fabric faces you. Iron the template to the up-facing back side of the first fabric in the stack.

3. Pin the stack so the fabric won't shift. Use very sharp scissors to cut the feathers, following the "top," "bottom," and "sides" guidelines shown by the feather patterns. (You don't have to be exact.) Remove the pin. You now have a stack of similar feathers.

4. If you've decided to use fabric as "skin" under the feathers in order to minimize the number of feathers you need to cut, take fabric pieces with values in the middle of your selected range and place them over the stabilizer in the feather areas. Make sure the skin doesn't extend over the edges of the beak and eyes.

> *Only the center of each feather is stitched, so that the feathers "flutter." This means that whatever is under the feathers can show. Make more feathers if you aren't using a fabric "skin" or if you want a fluffier look.* TIP

5. Follow the "top," "bottom," and "sides" guidelines (shown by the feather patterns) for placement around the eagle's face. Begin layering the feathers in one area at a time, overlapping them so no stabilizer shows when the edges are lifted slightly. Use as many pins as necessary to hold the feathers to each other and to the stabilizer before you move on to the next area.

6. Continue until all areas have been covered, checking often for color and value discrepancies. Slip the feathers closest to the beak and eyes under the face, as indicated by the dots on the feather guide (page 73).

Stitching

Basting with water-soluble basting thread lets you discard all the pins holding the feathers in place. This makes stitching the eye and beak area with the normal raw-edge method (page 57) much easier. The water-soluble basting thread will dissolve after you block your quilt (page 93).

> NOTE *When basting with water-soluble thread, you must use it both in the bobbin and on top.* Do not substitute!

1. If you use free-motion stitching to baste, use a large meander stitch across the entire feather area. You don't need to stitch the feathers individually; just make sure they are all caught and attached to the stabilizer/background. Remove the pins as you sew. Continue until no pins remain.

(If you don't do free-motion stitching, use the embroidery foot and stitch a large crosshatch stitch instead.)

Photo by Grace Errea

Detail from Rita Suthers' quilt top, shown in black and white, with water-soluble basting thread in place (full quilt, page 70).

2. Once the basting is complete, sew the eye/beak area with nylon thread, using the raw-edge stitching technique explained for *Tuscan Sunset* (page 57).

The Finishing Touches

When you have finished stitching the eagle's face, turn to Celebrating Your Journey (page 87) for suggestions about edge treatments and quilting. Quilt the fabric feathers along a central vein with lateral shoots to simulate real feathers, as shown in Quilting Patterns (pages 91 and 92).

As pictured, *The Eagle* is bound in a Value 5 fabric that complements the feather color. Note that I blocked, squared up, and trimmed my quilt to 28½″ × 20″. The water-soluble thread disappears during blocking. See Finishing Touches (page 93) for more about blocking and squaring.

Birds *of* a Feather

Here are some student versions of *The Eagle*. This pattern leaves plenty of room for individual expression through the choice of feather colors. The constant—more or less—is the toned yellow in the beak.

Photo by Meridith Osterfeld

Made by Jean Impey

Photo by Meridith Osterfeld

Made by Merci Apodaca

Photo by Grace Errea

Made by Pam Peeler

Photo by Grace Errea

Made by Marian Thurman

Photo by Grace Errea

Made by Judy Laird

Photo by Grace Errea

Made by Rita Suthers

For Further Inspiration

AMERICAN TREASURE, 27" × 30", by Grace Errea

This three-quarter view of a bald eagle head demonstrates how value can be used effectively with an impressionistic color palette. The feathers were stitched in place using the free-edge technique.

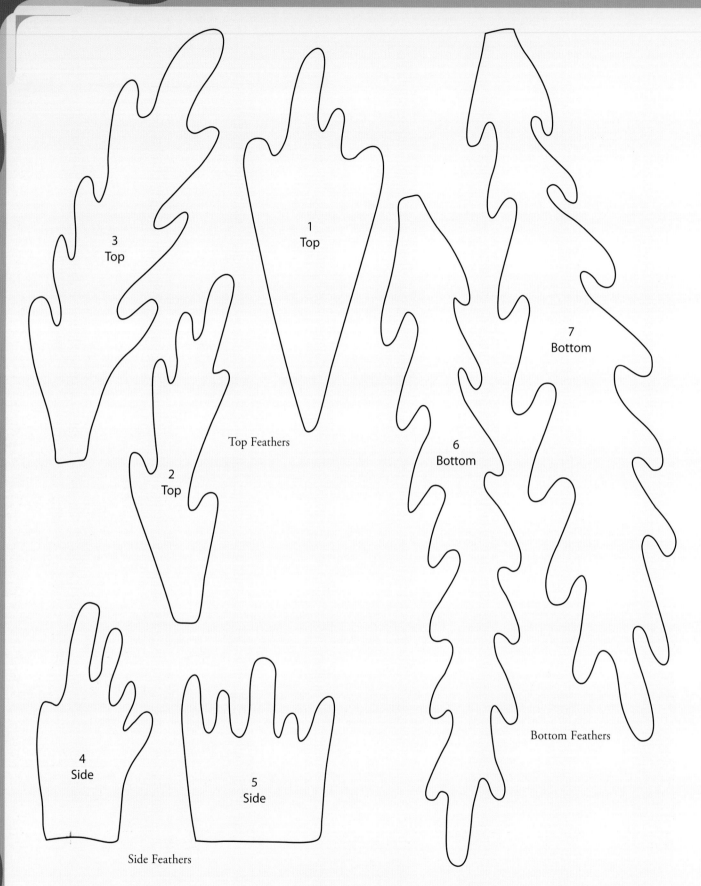

3
Top

1
Top

7
Bottom

2
Top

Top Feathers

6
Bottom

4
Side

5
Side

Bottom Feathers

Side Feathers

Pattern B: Feathers—Layer the fabric to cut the feathers in stacks. The same shapes are used for left-facing and right-facing feathers. Pieces 1, 2, and 3 are top right feathers; Pieces 4 and 5 are side feathers; and Pieces 6 and 7 are bottom right feathers. Turn the fabric over and they become left feathers.

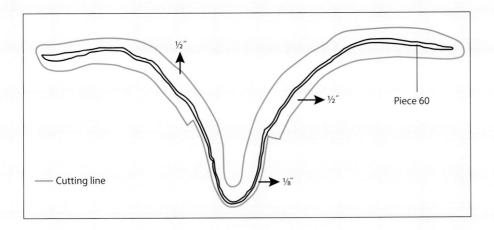

½″

½″

Piece 60

—— Cutting line

⅛″

Mouth guide

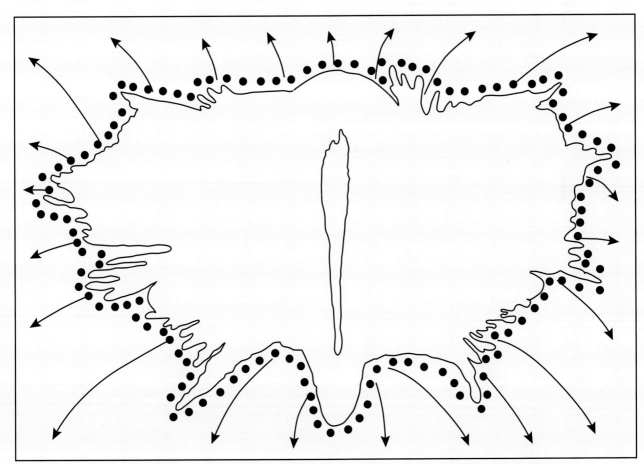

Feather guide—Dots show feather insertion points, and arrows indicate what directions to angle the feathers.

MELODIC SWAN, by Grace Errea in three hues—MOONLIGHT SERENADE, TAMALE TANGO, and MEADOW WALTZ, each 18¼″ × 28½″, including border and binding

As the sun sets, we reach the high point in our journey—a beautiful alpine meadow surrounding a crystal mountain lake. Gliding across the lake are majestic white swans. *Melodic Swan* emphasizes value as the primary element and color as secondary in a quilt's composition. It also focuses on the use of value to create a reflection.

The image of the swan and the swan's reflection in the lake are interpreted as if seen in three different light settings. The resulting art pieces reflect the colors of a moonlit night in *Moonlight Serenade*, the setting sun in *Tamale Tango*, and dawn's light (with the reflection modified by the green of the meadow and the trees on the water) in *Meadow Waltz*.

These quilts use two appliqué techniques: turned-edge appliqué (for the outer portions of the swan's head, the outer portions of the neck, and the back above the water line) and raw-edge appliqué (for the remaining portions of the neck, the body, and the reflection). In addition to showing how to use value to create a reflection, this project introduces the use of tulle to adjust a fabric's value and hue.

Fabric Requirements

The swan—You can use any color for the swan, provided you adhere to the values indicated on the master pattern (pullout page P–6).

Choose your color and gather as many fat quarters and smaller scraps in that one color family as possible. The fabrics should include tone-on-tone patterns in many values, from light to medium. Audition your fabrics to make sure there is good contrast between the swan and the background.

Beak and eye—The swan's beak and eye are both made from the same hue, in several values. The beak comprises Pieces 20–25, and the beak and eye reflection are Pieces 60 and 66–69. For the tiny pieces at the center of the swan's eye, use the values and hues indicated in the enlarged version of the

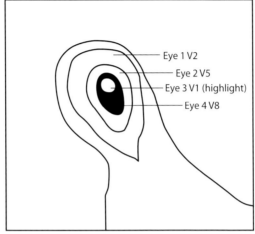

Enlarged close-up of the eye

pattern (above, right). Cut the eye pieces as solid shapes (not rings), starting with the outermost piece and working in to the center dot.

The beaks and eyes in *Moonlight Serenade*, *Tamale Tango*, and *Meadow Waltz* were created in colors that are the complements of the swans' bodies to provide a pleasing contrast (blue and gold, red and green, green and orange-yellow).

Tulle—If you don't have just the right fabrics in your stash, you may need small pieces of tulle in light, medium, and dark values to achieve the correct value and tonality for the reflection. Select tulle in the hues of the water and the swan. You won't know if you will need the tulle until you have assembled the swan (page 77).

Background, borders, and binding—You need 1 yard of Value 7–8 fabric to use for the 17″ × 26″ background, the border, and the binding. To make the border as shown, cut 1½″ strips for the top and sides and a 2½″ strip for the bottom.

Flange—To create the three-dimensional flange that frames the swan, you need ⅛ yard of Value 3–5 fabric in the same color as the swan. Cut 4 strips 1″ wide.

SUPPLIES

See Essential Supplies (page 20) for additional information and basic equipment.

Foam core board, 40″ × 30″

Straight pins and 1″–1½″ extra-thin silk pins

Painter's multiuse tape or masking tape

Clear vinyl (such as a painter's drop cloth or a tablecloth, 1–2mm thick), 26″ × 17″ or larger

Black fine-point Sharpie permanent marker

Freezer-paper roll, 18″ wide

Black ballpoint pen

Blue and red erasable pencils

Stabilizer material (petticoat netting), 26″ × 17″ or larger

Scissors for fabric and paper

Craft knife

Stiletto

Spray starch

Cotton swabs

Fabric stiffener

Fabric glue

Nylon thread in clear and smoke color

Bobbin prefilled with clear nylon thread **or** 50-weight cotton thread in neutral colors (if bobbin doesn't accept nylon thread)

Creating Reflections

Keep in mind that reflections on water may be toned or colored by the water itself. To create the correct value and hue for the reflection, take into consideration both the value and hue of the focal point (the swan) and the value and hue of the water. Choose something in between to create a realistic reflection.

(For more on relections, see page 17.)

Pattern Instructions

Refer to pullout pattern page P–6.

Position the pattern on your background fabric so that it is flush with the left edge of the pattern. The background material will extend beyond the pattern on the top, right, and bottom edges, as indicated in the diagram.

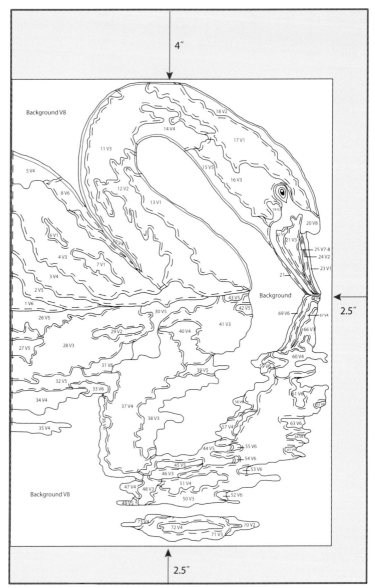

Pattern layout on background material

Creating *the* Vinyl Overlay, Pattern, *and* Pattern Notations

Refer to Making a Vinyl Overlay, (page 39) and Making Freezer-Paper Templates (page 40). To create the smooth, turned edges part of the quilt top, refer to Turned-Edge Appliqué (page 42). For the raw-edge pieces in the rest of the swan and in the reflection, see Raw-Edge Appliqué (page 55).

Pattern Notations

Mark the freezer-paper pattern with edge notations for turned and slide edges, using erasable blue pencil for the edges that slide under other pieces and erasable red pencil for the turned edges that go on top of other pieces.

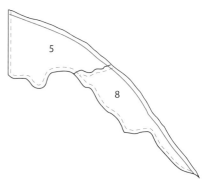

Blue dashed lines show where edges slide under other pieces, and solid red lines indicate turned edges.

Creating *the* Quilt Top

1. Place the stabilizer and background on your foam core board. Place the vinyl overlay, right side up, on top. Pin the vinyl overlay along the top edge.

2. Using freezer-paper templates, create the outer pieces of the head and neck, with smooth, turned edges, one at a time. As you complete each piece, position it on the background as indicated on the vinyl overlay.

3. Create the raw-edge pieces one at a time for the rest of the swan's body and the reflection. As you finish making each fabric piece, layer the pieces in place, starting from the top of the swan and working down to the water pieces and the pieces of the reflection. Use the head and neck as your starting point and the vinyl overlay as your guide.

4. Before stitching, view the quilt top without the vinyl overlay to check the values and hues of the entire composition. This is essential! During this critical step, I became aware that although the values in both the swan and the reflection were correct, the hue in the reflection needed adjustment. This is when I found I needed to go back and use tulle to alter the value of some of the pieces in the reflection.

5. When you are satisfied with the values, tone, and hue, stitch all the shapes of the quilt top with nylon thread.

One problem I encountered when working with reflections was the need to make them two values darker *for light swans on a dark background or two values* lighter *for dark swans on a light background. My stash lacked the properly toned fabrics, so I corrected this by using multiple layers of different-colored tulle over the fabric.* TIP

Photo by Dan Snipes

BLACK KNIGHT, 46″ × 33″, by Grace Errea

In *Black Knight,* the swan's reflection on the tinted and grayed water is three values lighter than the swan itself. The original reflection was too dark, so it was modified by adding layers of gray and white tulle.

Modifying Value with Tulle

If you need to adjust the value of the reflection after the quilt top is stitched with nylon thread, but you don't have the right fabrics in your stash, here's one solution:

1. Select tulle in several values in the same hues as the water and the swan. Layer several pieces over the entire reflection and pin in place.

2. Stand back and examine the quilt from 3–6 feet away. Add or remove tulle layers as necessary to get the hue and value you want.

3. Once you feel that the reflection is correct, use nylon thread to stitch the tulle in place, stitching only the outside edges of the reflection.

4. Trim the tulle up to the stitching line.

The Finishing Touches

Once you have completed the quilt top assembly, see Celebrating Your Journey (page 87) for tips on finishing your quilt. *Melodic Swan* is shown with one asymmetrical border and a three-dimensional accent piece—a flange—stitched into the seam between the quilt top and the border. The border and the binding are the same fabric as the background. The quilt top was squared up to 16¼″ × 25½″ before adding the border. The flange strips were cut 1″ wide. The top and side borders were cut to 1½″ wide, and the bottom border was cut to 2½″ wide. After blocking, the quilt was squared and trimmed to 18¼″ × 28½″. For more on blocking and squaring your quilt, see Finishing Touches (page 93).

For Further Inspiration

SWAN LAKE, 51″ × 37″, by Grace Errea

Using the same raw-edge and turned-edge appliqué techniques as *Melodic Swan*, this quilt shows a swan gliding across a lake in a more elaborate natural setting. The swan and its image as mirrored on the surface of the water could be created in any color, following the same value principles as for *Melodic Swan*.

Photo by Dan Snipes

POPSICLE SUNSET, 37½" × 29½", by Grace Errea

Photo by Dan Snipes

CREAMSICLE DAWN, 37½" × 29½", by Grace Errea

As our adventure comes to a close, the trail winds down to a secluded seaside cove where we capture the image of a spectacular sunset on the beach, followed by a serene dawn. *Popsicle Sunset* and *Creamsicle Dawn* are "painterly" representations that reinforce the way value within color families can change the entire feeling expressed in a quilt. The scene is exactly the same in both quilts. However, the darker shades in *Sunset* and the lighter tints in *Dawn* render the scene in completely different moods. Both quilts use turned-edge appliqué, giving the sky and the waves a smooth, realistic look.

The challenge here is twofold: selecting the proper values to achieve the painterly effect, and dealing with the many shapes needed to achieve a three-dimensional perspective and to set the mood in this large art piece.

SUPPLIES

See Essential Supplies (page 20) for additional information.

Foam core board, 40″ × 30″

Straight pins and extra-thin silk pins

Painter's tape

Clear vinyl (such as a painter's drop cloth or a tablecloth, 1–2mm thick)—2 pieces at least 40″ × 20″ each for the sky and the water, plus 1 piece at least 12″ × 12″ for the sun

Black fine-point Sharpie permanent marker

Fabric glue (Roxanne's Glue-Baste-It)

Freezer-paper roll, 18″ wide

Black ballpoint pen

Blue and red erasable pencils

Stabilizer material (petticoat netting), 30″ × 38″ or larger

Craft knife

Stiletto

Spray starch

Cotton swabs

Long-handled tweezers

Nylon thread in clear and smoke color

Bobbin prefilled with clear nylon thread **or** 50-weight cotton thread in neutral colors (if bobbin doesn't accept nylon thread)

79

Fabric Requirements

To reproduce the painterly effect of this art piece, it is important that you choose the values and colors shown in the chart for each piece. Choose fat quarters and smaller pieces of tone-on-tone fabrics in a range of values in the hues shown for either *Popsicle Sunset* or *Creamsicle Dawn*. For the sand on the beach, which is made up of Pieces 24, 27, 33, and 28, you need a traditional ¼ yard or more (*not* a fat quarter) of a "sand" type of fabric. This large piece acts as a background for the other beach pieces, so you don't have to cut each piece separately.

Popsicle/Creamsicle Values and Colors

TOP SHAPES

Piece	Creamsicle Value	Creamsicle Color	Popsicle Value	Popsicle Color	Piece	Creamsicle Value	Creamsicle Color	Popsicle Value	Popsicle Color
1	V1	Yellow	V4	Yellow	20	V3	Orange	V4	Yellow
2	V2	Gray	V5	Violet	21	V1	Orange	V3	Red/Orange
3	V2	Violet	V6	Brown/Violet	22	V2	Yellow	V5	Orange
4	V3	Yellow	V4	Yellow	23	V3	Orange	V6	Orange
5	V1	Yellow/Pink	V3	Yellow	24	V3	Violet	V6	Red/Violet
6	V3	Orange	V5	Orange	25	V2	Yellow	V5	Orange
7	V2	Orange	V4	Orange	26	V5	Orange	V6	Red
8	V3	Blue	V3	Orange	27	V5	Yellow	V6	Red
9	V5	Blue	V5	Violet	28	V5	Blue	V6	Violet/Blue
10	V3	Blue	V4	Orange	29	V4	Violet/Gray	V6	Red/Violet
11	V3	Yellow	V3	Yellow	30	V1	Orange	V3	Yellow
12	V3	Blue	V4	Yellow	31	V2	Yellow	V2	Yellow
13	V1	Orange	V3	Orange	32	V4	Gray	V6	Violet
14	V2	Orange	V5	Orange	33	V2	Gray	V4	Yellow
15	V5	Yell/Orange	V3	Orange	34	V5	Blue/Gray	V7	Violet
16	V4	Yellow	V4	Red	35	V4	Violet/Gray	V6	Red/Violet
17	V4	Orange	V4	Orange	36	V2	Orange	V5	Orange
18	V3	Orange	V4	Yellow	37	V4	Orange	V6	Red
19	V2	Yellow	V3	Yellow					

SUN SHAPES

Piece	Creamsicle Value	Creamsicle Color	Popsicle Value	Popsicle Color	Piece	Creamsicle Value	Creamsicle Color	Popsicle Value	Popsicle Color
1	V4	Yellow	V2	Yellow	6	V1	Off-white	V1	Off-white
2	V1	Off-white	V1	Off-white	7	V1	Off-white	V1	Off-white
3	V4	Yellow	V3	Yellow	8	V1	Off-white	V1	Off-white
4	V1	Yellow/Pink	V2	Yellow	9	V2	Violet	V3	Violet
5	V3	Yellow	V2	Yellow					

BOTTOM SHAPES

Piece	Creamsicle Value	Creamsicle Color	Popsicle Value	Popsicle Color	Piece	Creamsicle Value	Creamsicle Color	Popsicle Value	Popsicle Color
1	V7	Violet	V7	Violet	44	V1	Green	V2	Orange
2	V1	White	V1	White	45	V3	Yellow	V4	Yellow
3	V7	Blue	V7	Blue	46	V4	Yellow	V5	Yellow
4	V2	Blue/Green	V1	Violet	47	V1	Cream	V1	Cream
5	V5	Orange	V5	Yellow	48	V5	Red	V5	Red
6	V5	Blue/Green	V7	Blue	49	V4	Orange	V2	Yellow
7	V6	Blue	V6	Red	50	V3	Blue	V5	Orange
8	V4	Green	V7	Yellow/Brown	51	V3	Orange	V6	Violet/Blue
9	V4	Blue	V4	Orange	52	V1	White	V1	White
10	V4	Green	V4	Yellow	53	V2	Orange	V3	Orange
11	V5	Green/Blue	V3	Orange	54	V3	Violet	V2	Blue/Violet
12	V6	Blue/Green	V5	Red	55	V3	Blue	V5	Violet
13	V2	Orange	V6	Green	56	V1	White	V1	White
14	V4	Orange	V6	Orange	57	V1	Yellow	V1	Violet
15	V2	Blue	V6	Orange	58	V7	Blue	V7	Violet
16	V1	White	V1	White	59	V1	White	V1	White
17	V1	Violet	V1	Violet	60	V5	Yellow	V5	Yellow
18	V4	Blue/Green	V6	Green/Blue	61	V5	Orange	V6	Red
19	V3	Sand	V3	Sand	62	V1	White	V1	White
20	V5	Blue/Green	V7	Blue	63	V6	Blue	V7	Blue
21	V5	Violet	V6	Violet	64	V1	Cream	V1	Cream
22	V5	Orange	V5	Violet	65	V1	Green	V1	Orange
23	V5	Blue/Green	V4	Violet	66	V1	Blue/Violet	V1	Orange
24	V2	Sand	V2	Sand	67	V4	Blue/Violet	V6	Green
25	V6	Blue	V5	Violet	68	V5	Blue/Green	V7	Blue
26	V5	Orange	V7	Yellow/Brown	69	V2	Blue	V6	Orange
27	V2	Sand	V2	Sand	70	V7	Blue	V7	Blue
28	V2	Sand	V2	Sand	71	V4	Blue/Green	V6	Green
29	V1	White	V1	White	72	V1	White	V1	White
30	V5	Violet	V6	Violet	73	V3	Orange	V4	Violet
31	V6	Violet	V7	Violet	74	V5	Orange	V6	Orange
32	V2	Violet	V4	Violet	75	V1	White	V1	White
33	V3	Sand	V2	Sand	76	V1	White	V1	White
34	V5	Blue/Green	V6	Violet	77	V2	Cream	V5	Orange
35	V1	White	V1	White	78	V4	Blue/Violet	V7	Violet
36	V1	White	V1	White	79	V3	Yellow	V3	Yellow
37	V5	Blue/Green	V7	Green	80	V1	White	V4	Orange
38	V5	Blue/Green	V5	Orange	81	V3	Orange	V5	Orange
39	V4	Yellow	V4	Yellow	82	V6	Blue/Violet	V7	Blue
40	V1	Green	V3	Yellow	83	V3	Blue/Green	V4	Orange
41	V1	Green	V4	Yellow	84	V1	White	V1	White
42	V1	White	V1	White	85	V4	Orange	V5	Orange
43	V1	White	V1	White	86	V3	Blue/Green	V3	Green/Blue

You need ½ yard of fabric for the binding. For Popsicle Sunset, the binding is a Value 6–7, predominantly orange fabric.

For Creamsicle Dawn, it is a Value 6 fabric, also predominantly orange.

Setting the Mood

Here are key points to remember about using value to establish the mood you want:

- Tints versus shades can create entirely different moods for the same image or scene.

- Strong saturation and warm hues command more attention and elicit stronger emotions than do cooler, toned hues.

For more on setting the mood and time of day, see Establishing Time of Day and Conveying a Mood (page 18).

Pattern Instructions

Popsicle Sunset and *Creamsicle Dawn* are made from the same patterns: A and B. Pattern A is split into two pieces from top to bottom to fit on the page (see pullout pages P–4 and P–5). There are two major components of Pattern A: the sky and the water/sand. Join the two master pattern pieces for the sky/water/sand along the pattern join lines to make the full pattern. The sky (at the top) and the water/sand (at the bottom) come together to form a complete horizon line, shown with a thicker line at their interface. For ease while working on this large quilt top, divide the joined pattern at the horizon line, and then create and stitch the pieces of each component independently. You will then join them along the horizontal interface.

Pattern B (page 86)—the sun—is created separately and then appliquéd on top of the sky.

All the shapes are made using turned-edge appliqué. There are no edge notations on the master pattern pieces. You will determine which edges are turned (mark these with solid red lines) and which are slide edges (mark with blue dashed lines) based on two considerations: First is the location of the edge. The top edge of a shape is usually turned to cover the lower (slide) edge of the piece above; the bottom edge is generally a slide edge that will be covered by the next piece down. The second consideration is the shape's value. Lighter values usually slide under darker values.

Using the traditional layering method—that is, working from top to bottom—will help guide you in making your edge determinations.

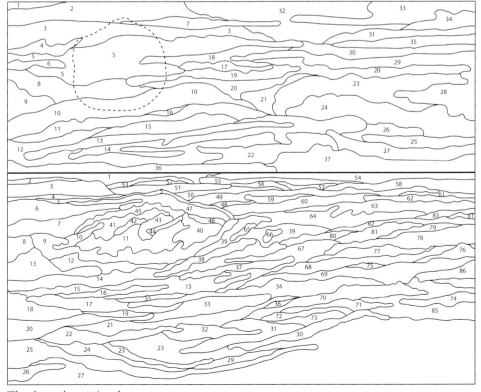

The sky and water/sand

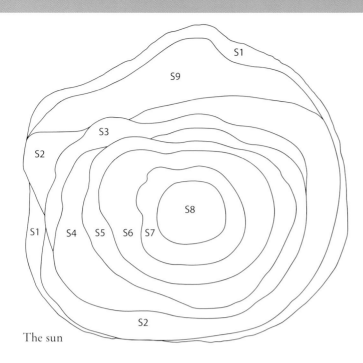

The sun

Creating the Quilt Top

Refer to Making a Vinyl Overlay (page 39), Making Freezer-Paper Templates (page 40), and Turned-Edge Appliqué (page 42) to create your quilt top.

1. Create 3 separate vinyl overlays: 1 for the sky portion of the master pattern, 1 for the water/sand portion of the master pattern, and 1 for the sun. Mark the position of the sun on the sky vinyl overlay.

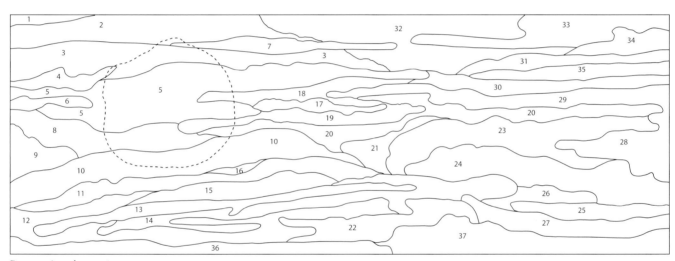

Pattern A—sky section

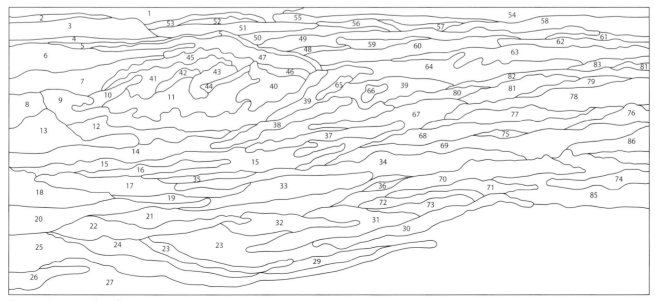

Pattern A—water/sand section

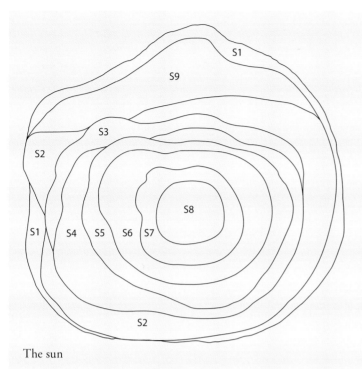

The sun

2. Make 3 corresponding freezer-paper patterns, one at a time. Be sure to double the freezer paper to make a stiffer set of templates for the turned-edge appliqué templates. Use the table (pages 80–81) to mark the templates with the appropriate value numbers. For edge notations, review "overies" and "undies" (see Pattern Notations and Instructions, page 38).

3. Starting with the top of Pattern A (the sky section), follow the traditional sequence to cut out the fabric pieces, turn the edges, and place the shapes over stabilizer on the foam core board under the vinyl overlay. Start at the top edge of the quilt, placing shapes as you work your way down. In general, each new shape's turned edges will cover the bottom slide edge of the piece (or pieces) above it. When all the pieces are in place, stitch around all the edges with nylon thread.

4. Create a vinyl overlay and freezer-paper templates for Pattern B (the sun). Cut out the fabric pieces as solid shapes (rather than rings), turn the edges, and stack and pin the layers, bottom to top, on a separate piece of stabilizer. Stitch the edges of each layer to the stabilizer using nylon thread. Trim the stabilizer close to the stitching.

5. Position the finished sun on top of the sky section, as indicated on the vinyl overlay. Stitch the sun to the background.

6. Assemble the water/sand portion on its own stabilizer, again working from top to bottom. Pay extra attention to making the turned edges on top as crisp and sharp as you can so that you will have a level horizon line.

7. Place the completed sky/sun and water/sand quilt top halves on the foam core board and pin in place. The turned top edges of the water/sand section will lie on top of the bottom raw edges of the sky section to form the horizon. *It is critical that the line that merges the pieces be level.* If the horizon isn't level, your quilt will not look realistic. Stitch the halves together.

After blocking, I squared up and trimmed my quilt to 37½″ × 29½″. After you have finished stitching together the quilt top, you'll find suggestions for applying the finishing touches to your quilt in Celebrating Your Journey (page 87).

For Further Inspiration

Photo by Dan Snipes

SUNSET ON THE BEACH, 82″ × 63″, by Grace Errea

One of the requests I frequently receive from my students is for a simplified version of this award-winning quilt, which contains hundreds of pieces in a variety of hues and values. By combining some shapes and making the quilt smaller, I was able to create *Popsicle Sunset* and *Creamsicle Dawn*. I narrowed the beach and eliminated the craggy rock on the right side. *Sunset on the Beach,* and the smaller versions *Popsicle Sunset* and *Creamsicle Dawn*, use turned-edge appliqué and illustrate the concept of joining together multiple pattern sections.

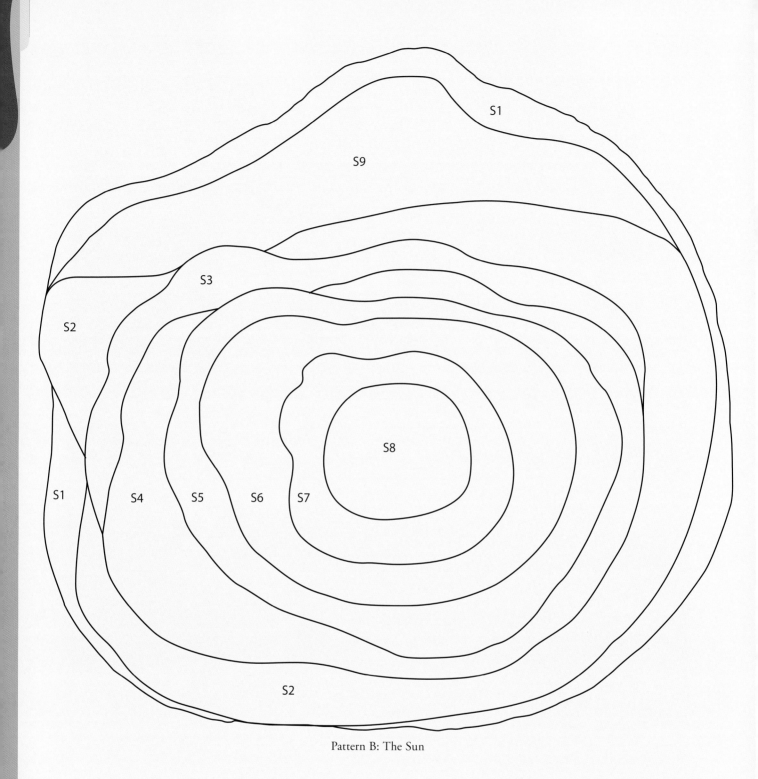

S1

S9

S3

S2

S1

S4   S5   S6   S7   S8

S2

Pattern B: The Sun

W-H-O-O'S THERE?, 27" × 34", by Grace Errea

Celebrating *Your* Journey

Congratulations! You've successfully navigated the trail and are on the road to becoming an art quilter. Creating an art quilt is a major accomplishment, and every art piece deserves to be properly framed for display. The suggestions in this chapter are designed to help you put the final touches on your artwork.

THE WHO FAMILY PORTRAIT, 43" × 35", by Grace Errea

On *the* Edge

Bordering or binding is a matter of personal preference. Each quilt artist must decide what best frames his or her art piece. An edge can enhance the art piece or, conversely, detract from it. The edge can be an extension of the artwork or a place to stop the eye and bring the focus back to the composition. The edge should complement your art and enhance the design. The focal point must always remain the strongest element in the composition.

Hang your art quilt on a wall for several days. As you study it, ask yourself the following questions.

Border or Bind?

Does the quilt need a border, or will a binding accomplish the same objective?

Do you need to stop the viewer's eye and bring it back to the focal point by using a framelike border, or is the focus clear enough that a simple, minimalist binding will accomplish the same thing?

Glorious Morning is quite busy. A border helps emphasize the focal point and focus the viewer's attention. In this case, there is actually a double border, with a narrow flange sewn into the seam between the borders.

> # NOTE
> *A flange is simply a strip of fabric, folded in half, with its raw edges sewn into the seam and its folded edge left unstitched. Use your favorite method to add a flange.*

Glorious Morning, before and after bordering and binding

Photo by Dan Snipes

For *Life after the Storm,* I chose an entirely different tactic to get the viewer to examine the composition more closely. There are two subtle borders on the top and left side; the top border is a single piece incorporating colors from the quilt, while the left border is made from pieces of the quilt fabrics. A binding frames the quilt and is several values darker than the outside edges of the quilt top. On two sides (top and left), the binding completes the outer border that frames the quilt top. On the right side and bottom, there is no border, so the binding completes the quilt top. Also on the right side and bottom, a few leaves escape to finish the "frame" in a three-dimensional fashion.

LIFE AFTER THE STORM, 49" × 51", by Grace Errea

Should a Border Be Symmetrical?

Do the borders on your quilt need to be symmetrical?

Should they be the same width and the same color or pattern all the way around?

How wide should they be?

I do not subscribe to the idea that a quilt needs large identical and symmetrical borders on all sides. *Piano Hands* has asymmetrical borders to balance the keyboard and to keep the hands from appearing to float off the quilt. The flange helps frame the main composition.

PIANO HANDS, 44" × 29", by Grace Errea

THE WEBMASTER, 55" × 40", by Grace Errea

When looking at *The Webmaster*, you may be hard-pressed to identify any border other than the binding. You will see a narrow, earth-tone strip along the bottom of the quilt. What lies below that is a well-disguised border that continues the theme of the composition and "grounds" the tree and other plants. The tree on the left and the fronds on the right, though not true borders, serve as such for the "snapshot" of the spider.

What about Color and Fabric?

What color and fabric should you use for the border?

Color choice is crucial when it comes to bordering your quilt. If you do not see the color in the quilt, do not use it in the border!

You need to give some closure to your design. Borders in colors similar to those already present in the quilt will extend the artwork and allow it to flow into the border. Using a contrasting color in the border will stop the eye and clearly define the outer limits of the focal piece. Always use a color that is present in the quilt top, though it can be in a different fabric.

To frame a light- or middle-value composition, use borders that are two to three values darker. For a quilt with dark values, choose a lighter border.

If you want to add interest with multiple borders, use a very thin inner border and a slightly wider outer border. A thin strip for an inner border, even if it is only ½" wide, will stop the eye and keep it focused on the composition.

Block before binding. (See Pressing and Blocking, page 93.) TIP

Tying Up *the* Loose Ends

Backing and Batting

Always choose good-quality fabric for your backing. It will help your art piece hang flat, without stretching or distortion.

Thinner battings, such as Hobbs Heirloom Wool or Warm and Natural, are excellent choices for art quilts. Don't use any batting that has lots of loft or that includes polyester in its mix. The batting should be thin, flat, and lightweight to facilitate hanging. Also, polyester tends to "pill" on the outside of the quilt, which detracts from an art piece.

Quilting

Quilting is one of the final steps in the process of creating your art quilt. Here are some thoughts that may help you.

- I feel that quilting is simply a function of joining three layers: the quilt top, the batting, and the backing. With few exceptions, I do not use quilting as an additional artistic factor or embellishment for my quilts.

- Use 50-weight cotton thread, matching the color and value of the top thread to the color of the area you are quilting. For the bobbin, closely match the color and value of the top thread. Use thicker thread (40-weight or 30-weight) for areas you want to accent.

- If you use variegated thread, the colors must blend well with the area you are quilting. You can use rayon or metallic threads for occasional embellishment. A little goes a long way.

- Start and stop your stitching on the edges of the quilt where it won't show. If you can't do that, bury the tails of the thread in the quilt batting.

Quilting patterns

Botanicals, landscapes, and animal portraits are relatively simple to quilt. Observe nature and copy what you see in your quilting. Follow natural patterns in the fabric to suggest clouds in the sky, veins in leaves, water, grass, and other features.

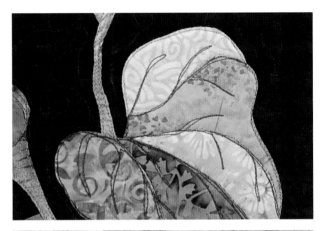

Follow nature's path to simulate veins on leaves and flowers.

Photos by Grace Errea

Try out a potential quilting pattern by drawing it on your quilt with a water-soluble pen. This works very well on light fabrics. Or test a design by drawing it on clear vinyl with a fine-point Sharpie permanent marker. Place the vinyl over the quilt top and stand back to inspect it. If you like the design, duplicate it with thread. If you don't, throw out the vinyl and start with a new design.

Quilting fills this sky with simulated clouds of various sizes.

For mountains, outline the major crests and then use quilting to suggest smaller hills leading up to them.

Water movement can be implied through little swirls and eddies.

Looking at the back of a quilt—in these two photos of *The Eagle*—is a good way to see the quilting pattern (full quilt on page 63).

Feathers in a quilt resemble leaves. A central quilting branch bisects the feather like a quill, with minor branches going outward at regular intervals.

Finishing Touches

Celebrate your accomplishments! These last few touches will ensure that your art quilt will be enjoyed for years to come.

Pressing and Blocking

Blocking is an important step to ensure that your art quilt will hang straight. You need a foam insulation board the size of the quilt or larger.

> *Foam insulation board is available at building supply stores in 4′ × 8′ and 4′ × 4′ sheets. This fairly inexpensive material comes in a variety of thicknesses. It's perfect for making a design space on a wall. Use a craft knife to cut the board, and then cover it with fabric or white paper if you wish.*
>
> TIP

1. Block a quilt after it is quilted but before the binding is attached. To block, use a dry iron to press on the back of the quilt. *Press only—do not iron back and forth!* If necessary, spritz lightly with a little water to "steam out" a pucker.

2. Use T-pins every 1″–2″ to pin the top edge of the quilt to the design wall or board. Stretch the top out to the side as you pin—the quilt needs to be taut and lie flat against the board. Repeat the process for the bottom edge, stretching the quilt downward as you pin.

3. Pin one side of the quilt, working first from the middle to the top edge and then from the middle to the bottom. Pull and gently stretch the side to keep it straight and taut as you work. Repeat on the opposite side.

Photo by Meridith Osterfeld

Flower pins were used here instead of the usual T-pins so that they would show up clearly in the photo.

4. Restretch and repin any areas that don't seem tight enough. Then spray the quilt with cool water to moisten it all the way through.

5. Let the quilt dry thoroughly. It may take several days, depending on the size of the quilt.

Squaring Up

Not every art quilt needs to be squared—some artists prefer an uneven appearance. But even if your art piece has irregular edges, you should square the top so the quilt will hang properly. Perfect corners and straight edges are helpful when your quilt is hung for display. Here's how to square it:

1. Place the quilt on a cutting mat and smooth it out. Using a rotary cutter and ruler, trim one side of the quilt, from the top corner to the bottom corner, so that it is perfectly straight.

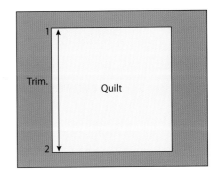

2. Using an L square or a large square quilt ruler and a long ruler against the already-trimmed edge, trim the top edge of the quilt.

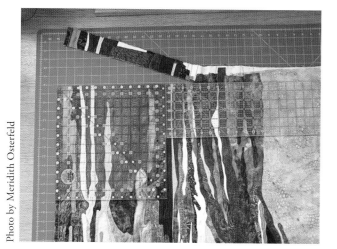

3. Measure in several places, both horizontally and vertically. Trim to square the remaining edges. Then measure again to make sure that nothing has become distorted. Trim as necessary.

Wrapping It Up

Use your favorite technique to bind the finished top and to apply a hanging sleeve on the back. Cut binding strips 2¼″ wide and join them to make a strip as long as the perimeter of the finished quilt, plus 10″ for turning corners and overlapping at the end. Fold the binding strip in half lengthwise and apply it to the edges of the quilt front, using a ¼″ seam allowance. Then turn and hand stitch the binding to the back of the quilt.

Be sure to sign your quilt. I sign mine in the lower right front corner, using a thread color that blends well. This becomes part of the permanent ID on the quilt.

Make a label with your name, location, and the date of completion and hand stitch it to the back of your quilt. If you have an extra appliqué piece that you didn't use on the quilt front, consider using it for your label.

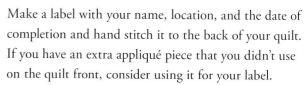

Storing

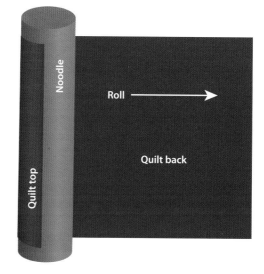

To prevent creases, roll your quilt on a foam swimming noodle to store it. Starting from the top, roll the quilt with the front facing out so that it will hang properly when unrolled and displayed. You can roll several quilts together, one on top of the other. Make a fabric "pillowcase" to cover the roll, and tie the end shut.

Photos by Michael Lee, Starlight Photography

Grace J. Errea

Meridith Osterfeld

Fiber artist, designer, and art quilter, Grace Errea began her quilting journey in 2000. Her art focuses on the depiction of inspiring scenes in a "value-based" contemporary-realistic manner. Grace's work has been recognized for its exceptional primary use of value and secondary use of color. Her innovative techniques and depiction of nature and people, in combination with her focus on value, have attracted widespread interest from the quilting world, as well as from national and international galleries, museums, and publications. When not quilting, Grace enjoys gardening and gourmet cooking. A mother of two, she lives in Southern California with her husband, Mack, and her cats, Thelma and Louise.

Meridith Osterfeld became involved in the quilting world in 2000, as a photographer, writer, and web master. An avid gardener, nature photographer, mom of four, and "Gramma" to nine, she found her creative niche in art quilting. When asked "Why art quilting?" she laughingly replies that she's always been the proverbial salmon swimming upstream, doing what others say couldn't or shouldn't be done. Art quilting, photography, gardening, and writing all inspire her to explore the creative world outside the box. Meridith lives with her husband, Hank, and her dog, Taupe, in Southern California.

Great Titles *from* C&T PUBLISHING and stashBOOKS®

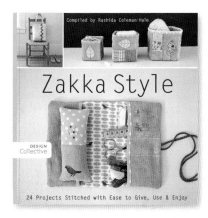

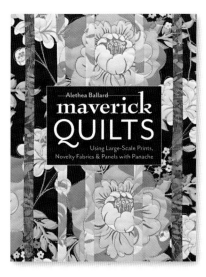

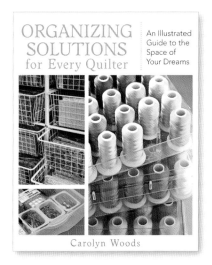

Available at your local retailer or **www.ctpub.com** *or* **800-284-1114**

For a list of other fine books from C&T Publishing, visit our website to view our catalog online.

C&T PUBLISHING, INC.

P.O. Box 1456
Lafayette, CA 94549
800-284-1114

Email: ctinfo@ctpub.com
Website: www.ctpub.com

C&T Publishing's professional photography services are now available to the public. Visit us at www.ctmediaservices.com.

Tips and Techniques can be found at www.ctpub.com > Consumer Resources > Quiltmaking Basics: Tips & Techniques for Quiltmaking & More

For quilting supplies:

COTTON PATCH

1025 Brown Ave.
Lafayette, CA 94549
Store: 925-284-1177
Mail order: 925-283-7883

Email: CottonPa@aol.com
Website: www.quiltusa.com

Note: Fabrics shown may not be currently available, as fabric manufacturers keep most fabrics in print for only a short time.